GOD's GLORY IN AN EARTHEN VESSEL

A STUDY OF THE BOOK OF JONAH

CHRISTY VOELKEL

Copyright © 2019 by Christy Voelkel

Scripture taken from the New King James Version®. Copyright © 1982 by Thomas Nelson. Used by permission. All rights reserved. Unless otherwise noted, all Scripture cited in this study is from the NKJV.

Scriptures passages have been copied from the online Bible reference source, Blue Letter Bible (www.blueletterbible.org) using its copy feature.

Strong's Hebrew Lexicon definitions from Blue Letter Bible. Web. 7 May, 2018.

Table of Contents

Introduction: God's Glory and the Earthen Vessel	1
Overview: The Book of Jonah	5

Part 1: The Earthen Vessel

Jonah 1: Jonah and God (Jonah 1:1-2)	11
Jonah 1: Jonah and the Sailors (Jonah 1:3-16) From the Sailors' Perspective	25
Jonah 1: Jonah and the Sailors (Jonah 1:3-16) From Jonah's Perspective	37
Jonah 2: Jonah and God, Again	51
Jonah 3: Jonah and the Ninevites From the Ninevites' Perspective	67
Jonah 4: Jonah and God, Again	77
Jewish Application of Jonah	89
Summary of the Earthen Vessel	99

Part 2: The Glory of God in the Earthen Vessel

Introduction: Seeing the Picture within the Picture	105
Deconstructing Jonah	109
Pictures of Christ in Jonah	
Scenario 1: A Prophet with a Ministry of Baptism	131
Scenario 2: Christ's Baptism	133
Scenario 3: Christ's Temptations	135
Scenario 4: A Man Asleep in a Boat in a Storm	137
Scenario 5: Christ's Death and Resurrection	138
Scenario 6: A Kingdom Lost	141
Scenario 7: The Grand Picture	148
Conclusion	153

INTRODUCTION

God's Glory and the Earthen Vessel

"For it is the God who commanded light to shine out of darkness, who has shone in our hearts to give the light of the knowledge of the glory of God in the face of Jesus Christ. But we have this treasure in earthen vessels, that the excellence of the power may be of God and not of us."
—2 Corinthians 4:6-7

The glory of God and an earthen vessel—what a magnificent contrast! Placed side by side, the immeasurable, indescribable glory of an almighty, majestic God becomes even more glorious while the clay vessel appears even more humble and fragile.

How appropriate that Paul uses the Greek word *ostrakinos*, meaning earthenware, when describing the clay of this vessel. Even among the grades of clay, this one is the least. It has none of the beauty, purity, or strength of porcelain. It doesn't even have the versatility or resilience of stoneware. Earthenware, also known as terracotta, is the most common clay used for making tiles, bricks, and flowerpots. It is brittle and chips easily under pressure. Its composition is so filled with impurities that only the least amount of firing can be used to mature it without melting it completely; and even after firing, the vessel remains porous, leaky, prone to staining, and ever so easily broken.

We are that earthen vessel—an earthen body full of impurities that even a refiner's fire cannot completely drive out of us. Without constant cleansing and a seal to protect us, we are easily stained, dirtied through and through, and unfit for service. We appear strong, but in truth we are fragile, quick to crumble under pressure, and so brittle that one sharp blow shatters us.

Before the fierce fire of God's holiness, we would melt. We are only able to stand before that fire and endure the melting away of our impurities because Christ first endured the fullness of that fire for us. The refining fire we now endure, and are able to endure, does not destroy us but strengthens us so that we might be of use in service to a holy God.

In the light of His purity, our impurities would disqualify us for His service if not for the continual cleansing we receive through Christ.

Under the weight of His majesty, we would be crushed, and yet He chooses not to crush us nor allow any other to crush us. He strengthens us with His own strength, so that we are *"hard-pressed on every side, yet not crushed; we are perplexed, but not in despair; persecuted, but not forsaken; struck down, but not destroyed."* (2 Corinthians 4:8-9)

Any strength, any purity, and any beauty manifested in the common clay of our humanity is solely because of the work of Jesus Christ and the indwelling Holy Spirit in our lives, to the glory of God the Father. Such earthenware would never grace a king's table, but it is that very vessel God chooses to fill with His glory.

If ever there was a study of contrasts between a glorious God and a man of clay, it is found in the book of Jonah. Jonah is the quintessential earthenware vessel. His character so full of flaws that not even a three-day stint in the belly of a fish can drive them from him. He typifies the worst of humanity in his selfishness, mercilessness, anger, and unfaithfulness. And yet, into the life of this hopelessly flawed man—into each act of obedience and even Jonah's moments of disobedience—the Lord draws the picture of a future Savior in all His glory. The full picture of Jesus' earthly ministry, from His baptism to His death and resurrection and beyond, plays out in the narrative picture in glorious detail.

The following is a study of the book of Jonah broken into two parts. Part 1 is an examination of the earthen vessel, the man of clay. We make a first pass through the book in an expository way, examining Jonah. The narrative of the book is broken up into very distinct sections, almost like acts in a theatrical play. As we walk through the text, we are looking at the events from Jonah's perspective; but we also step into the shoes of different characters—the sailors and Ninevites—to see the events through their eyes. The narrative yields additional applications when assessed from different perspectives.

I also include a brief chapter on how the book of Jonah is incorporated into Jewish understanding and practices. Seeing how Jesus' disciples applied the book of Jonah in their lives helps bring the book into a New Testament context.

In Part 2, we make a second pass through the book, focusing on the glorious picture of the Messiah that emerges through the narrative story. To do this, we deconstruct the narrative picture, study the individual pieces of imagery that become the building blocks for the larger picture, and then, using those building blocks, reassemble the picture to reveal the big picture of Israel and the Messiah in all its detail.

It is my hope that through this study of the Old Testament illustration of Jonah, you gain an appreciation for the marvelous truth Paul is teaching in 2 Corinthians 4:6-7. We, as believers, are earthen vessels in which God chooses to manifest His glory, so that the world will look at us and understand that the power in us is of God and not ourselves. If God's glory can shine through the life of such a flawed character as Jonah, none of us are without hope.

OVERVIEW

The Book of Jonah

It is always good to begin with some introductory discussion of a book—its author, its purpose, where it fits in context with other books of the Bible, and such. So here is a quick overview.

The Author and Historicity of Jonah

The book of Jonah is written in the objective, third person point of view, which has caused some scholarly debate over who is the author of the book. Jewish sources class this as a postexilic text written long after the events were past.[1] Other scholars think that Jonah narrates this himself because the story recounts emotions and events that only Jonah would have known. A few prophets such as Isaiah and Jeremiah write parts of their accounts in the third person, but the authorship is clear in those cases. Not so with Jonah. For this reason, some scholars consider Jonah to be an allegory.

An allegory is a story where a narrator creates an imaginary set of characters and events to teach a particular lesson. While the book of Jonah definitely has a moral point to make, its characters and events are not imaginary. This is what we know about Jonah from biblical, archeological, and other historical records:

- He is a prophet from Gath-hepher, a city in Zebulun, who lives during the reign of Jeroboam II and prophesies that Jeroboam II would retake the northern border of Israel on which the Assyrian provinces had been encroaching (2 Kings 14:25)—a prophecy that comes true. If this were an allegory, it wouldn't be tied to historical figures or events on a historical timeline.

- Nineveh is also a very real place and the Ninevites, very real people. There are differing opinions as to when Jonah's mission to Nineveh takes place, but historical and archeological records suggest he is sent to Nineveh during the reign of Ashur-dan III, which we talk about

---

[1] Berlin, A. and Brettler, M. (2004). The Jewish Study Bible, Jewish Publication Society Tanakh translation. New York, New York: Oxford University Press. p 1199.

in some detail. A gravesite attributed to Jonah (called Nebi Yunus) has been found in the archeological site of Nineveh. Who makes a gravesite for an allegorical person?

- Jesus speaks of Jonah and the Ninevites as real people. When Jesus rebukes the Jewish leaders of His day, He points to Jonah's prophecy as a sign that He will rise from the dead after three days, and He uses the Ninevites as examples of true repentance, saying that they will rise at the judgment and condemn that wicked generation (Matthew 12:39-41).

The people in this book are real, the places are real, and the events connect to a real historical timeline. Therefore, we know that the book of Jonah is not an allegory. We are dealing with a real person and one to whom we can relate. It is, however, difficult to pin this period of his life to a place on the historical timeline. Apart from the reference to Jeroboam II, we are left to figure out when these events take place based on suppositions drawn from events recorded in Assyrian historical records.

The narrative describes events on several levels. There are actual events that unfold in the lives of the characters in their time. There is a prophetic picture of events on a near horizon for the northern kingdom of Israel in the illustration of the vine and the worm, which I explain, and there is the sign of Jonah that identifies a future Messiah.

Jonah as a Prophet

In the pantheon of prophets, Jonah takes his place early. The prophets Elijah and Elisha precede him. Amos and Hosea are his contemporaries. Isaiah and rest of the prophets of the exile and postexilic era follow him.

Jonah is a prophet from the northern kingdom of Israel. Jonah, Amos, and Hosea are the prophets who arise at the time when Israel and Assyria's timelines are preparing to merge as the Lord sends the northern kingdom of Israel into captivity. Jonah is sent to the Ninevites to prepare them as God's agents of discipline while Amos and Hosea are sent to Israel with fair warning of the coming exile.

Jonah is a tested prophet. His prophecy concerning Jeroboam II comes true, and so we know he is the real deal as far as prophets go. He has the distinction of being the only Hebrew prophet sent to a Gentile nation. Other prophets like Daniel find themselves captive in Gentile nations, and they prophesy to those kings and peoples. Jonah, on the other hand, is asked to voluntarily leave Israel and go to a Gentile nation. Perhaps the only other prophet sent to a foreign nation like this is Elijah, who is sent to Damascus to anoint Hazael as King of Syria (1 Kings 19:15).

There are two ways prophets get God's message across. One way is by speaking prophecies that God gives them to speak. The other is by acting in a way that God tells them to act, so that people look at them and ask, "What are you doing? Why are you doing that?" In both cases, God usually gives the prophet an interpretation of the action with which to answer the people.

This book is not about Jonah's spoken prophecies. Jonah makes only two prophetic statements in the entire narrative: 1) in Jonah 1:12, he tells the sailors the sea will become calm if they throw him over, which it does, and 2) in Jonah 3:4, he tells the Ninevites, *"Yet forty days, and Nineveh shall be overthrown!"* God's message is delivered not so much through Jonah's spoken prophecy as through the actions of the prophet himself as he lives out a lesson. Unlike other prophets, God doesn't give Jonah instructions on what to do or the interpretation of it. God does something unique in that He allows Jonah's own inclination and choices to dictate the flow of events without Jonah realizing that God is making a lesson out of him.

The lesson isn't really for the people of Jonah's time, though. The sailors don't know what happens after they threw Jonah in the sea. They give him up for dead. The Ninevites don't witness what happened on the ship. None of them know of the dialogue that goes on between Jonah and God at the end. All of these events takes place away from Israel, and it doesn't appear that Jonah ever returns to Israel, as his grave is in Nineveh. So, for whom is this lesson really?

The real picture that plays out in the life of Jonah is a portrayal of a coming Messiah. His message was a sign for the Jews of Jesus' day, and his life is a lesson for us even today.

Yet Jonah isn't a character with whom we may wish to identify. As we read through his account, we come to the understanding pretty quickly that Jonah is going be one of those bad examples we find in Scripture. What does he think he is doing? Why does he do that? (You can't help but ask those kinds of questions.) Then we say to ourselves, "I wouldn't have acted that way." In this we deceive ourselves, because we *do* act that way. We are all earthen vessels with intrinsically flawed characters. As we work through the lessons and examine why Jonah does what he does, I hope that you have some moments of self-assessment and conviction, even as I had when I taught this book. I think this is why Jonah's narrative was so pointedly written in the voice of the third-person observer, to give us that raw objective view of what our own humanity looks like.

The Narrative Structure

The Book of Jonah has a very distinctive narrative structure. Jonah interacts with two sets of Gentiles (the sailors and the Ninevites), and each interaction follows a parallel structure.

Jonah & God . . . Jonah & the sailors . . . The sailors & God (Jonah 1:1-16)
Jonah & God . . . Jonah & the Ninevites . . .The Ninevites & God (Jonah 1:17-3:10)
Jonah & God (Jonah 4)   (end of narrative)

The book begins and ends with a dialogue between Jonah and God, which creates a sort of inclusio for the narrative sandwiched in between. While the sailors and Ninevites are a significant part of the lesson, they are cast more in the role of God's tools for dealing with Jonah. The overall thrust of the narrative is Jonah's relationship with God.

The interplay between God and Jonah throughout the book presents a micro view of Israel's history—her waxing and waning relationship with God up through the time of Christ. Jonah 1-3 describes in very broad strokes Israel's history until Christ's first advent. Jonah 4 illustrates Israel's face-to-face interaction with God as He comes in person to confront His wayward children, carrying the picture through Christ's earthly ministry and even beyond His death.

The narrative of Jonah ends abruptly with the Lord's rebuke, leaving the act of Israel's final turning of heart in question and her narrative unfinished. We examine all this in the second half of this study, but let us first begin with Jonah himself, the earthen vessel.

PART ONE

The Earthen Vessel

Jonah 1: Jonah and God

JONAH 1:1-2

"Now the word of the LORD came to Jonah the son of Amittai, saying, 'Arise, go to Nineveh, that great city, and cry out against it; for their wickedness has come up before Me.' But Jonah arose to flee to Tarshish from the presence of the LORD." —Jonah 1:1-2

Jonah is a prophet of God. He has one prophecy under his belt already and it was good news for Jeroboam II—that Jeroboam would take back the land on which the Assyrians had been encroaching.

The fact that Jeroboam needs to take the land back from the Assyrians hints at one of the reasons for Jonah's abhorrence of them. Assyria is an up-and-coming world empire, exceedingly aggressive and brutal in their dealings with conquered territories, and they are a national threat to Israel.

It's great to be the prophet proclaiming good news; not so great when the news is bad. It is one thing to make a pronouncement against Assyria when you are standing behind a king and an army who are assured of victory. It is another thing to go by yourself into enemy territory and make the same pronouncement without the protection of a king and an army or assurance of safety.

Yet that is what God does to Jonah in sending him to Nineveh. He sends a Hebrew prophet to a Gentile nation with bad news of their impending judgment, but it is bad news meant to bring about a people's turning. We know from reading further in the book that as a result of Jonah's message, the Ninevites have a change of heart and repent. In a future generation, God wipes out Assyria, but for this generation that repents He offers mercy. So in reality, God sends Jonah to be an ambassador of mercy.

In being sent as God's ambassador to a heathen nation, Jonah fits into a very particular type of ambassador found in Scripture called a *tsiyr* (pronounced like tsar, but with an "e"—tseer.) When we think of ambassadors, we tend to think of goodwill ambassadors who make peace accords. The *tsiyr* is not that kind of ambassador. He is an ambassador who is sent not to make peace, but to stir things up. Let's sketch a quick understanding of the character of the *tsiyr*.

The Tsiyr

I list some verses below where the *tsyir* is mentioned in the Bible, and we can deduce something of the nature of this ambassador from these verses.

> *"Woe to the land shadowed with buzzing wings, which is beyond the rivers of Ethiopia, which sends ambassadors **[tsiyr]** by sea, even in vessels of reed on the waters, saying, 'Go, swift messengers, to a nation tall and smooth of skin, to a people terrible from their beginning onward, a nation powerful and treading down, whose land the rivers divide.'"—Isaiah 18:1-2*

In the greater context of this passage, these ambassadors are envoys sent by kings ahead of invading armies, who give the people a chance to capitulate before war breaks out. This same picture is found in Obadiah 1:1-2.

> *"'For I have sworn by Myself,' says the LORD, 'that Bozrah shall become a desolation, a reproach, a waste, and a curse. And all its cities shall be perpetual wastes.' I have heard a message from the LORD, and an ambassador **[tsiyr]** has been sent to the nations: 'Gather together, come against her, and rise up to battle! For indeed, I will make you small among nations, despised among men.'"—Jeremiah 49:13-15*

These ambassadors are sent to stir things up. In Jonah's case, he is going to deliver the message against Nineveh; but in God's big plan, Jonah is actually prepping Nineveh to come against Israel.

These verses describe the ambassador, but *tsiyr* is not just translated as ambassador in Scripture. *Tsiyr* also describes the nature of the message these ambassadors bring. It is a painful message likened to labor pains. Just as labor pains begin with that initial shock of pain and then you know what is coming, so *tsiyr* are painful messages that herald imminent judgment.

> *"Wail, for the day of the LORD is at hand! It will come as destruction from the Almighty. Therefore all hands will be limp, every man's heart will melt, and they will be afraid. Pangs **[tsiyr]** and sorrows will take hold of them; They will be in pain as a woman in childbirth..."—Isaiah 13:6-8*

> *"Therefore my loins are filled with pain; Pangs **[tsiyr]** have taken hold of me, like the pangs of a woman in labor. I was distressed when I heard it; I was dismayed when I saw it."—Isaiah 21:3*

> *"And suddenly, one having the likeness of the sons of men touched my lips; then I opened my mouth and spoke, saying to him who stood before me, 'My lord, because of the vision my sorrows **[tsiyr]** have overwhelmed me, and I have retained no strength.'"—Daniel 10:16*

What eventually comes as a result of the labor pains is a good thing, but you have to go through the pain to receive the benefit. In the same way, the *tsiyr's* message brings pain but in the end produces health. And so we see in the proverbs:

> "A wicked messenger falls into trouble, but a faithful ambassador **[tsiyr]** brings health."—Proverbs 13:17

This is Jonah in a nutshell. He is the messenger who doesn't want to be a messenger, and he is going to get into trouble when he fails in his duty as ambassador. But when he finally gets around to delivering the message, the message—while painful to hear—brings spiritual health to the people of Nineveh. And in the long run, it is going to bring health to the nation of Israel.

The Mission

God gives Jonah the command to go to Nineveh, and Jonah gets up and heads in the other direction. Jonah is unique in that he is the only prophet to run away from God. Some prophets balk at God's requests, some argue, others weep, but only Jonah actually flees from God.

Jonah doesn't just go in the opposite direction; he goes as far away as he can get from Israel and Nineveh in the opposite direction. Scholars differ on where Tarshish was located, but the general consensus seems to be that it was somewhere around the tip of Spain. It was the end of the known world for ships that ply the Mediterranean Sea. Jonah boards a boat bound for the far side of the sea to get away from God and the mission.

It isn't just an issue that Jonah has with the Ninevites at this point. He could stay in Israel and not deal with the Ninevites. So why leave Israel? To get away from God. Jonah has two issues really. One is with the Ninevites, and the other is with God. The issue with God is what is driving him to Tarshish.

Ninevites in Our Lives

Sometimes the Lord sends us to people in other countries on a mission trip, but sometimes they are nearer to home. Sometimes He sends us to people we don't know much about; sometimes we know a lot about them—too much, really. Sometimes we have a bad history with them, and we do not want to go because of that history. Maybe they are cruel and abusive. Maybe they are so deeply into a particular worldly lifestyle that we figure there is no hope they will ever change. They may be in enmity to God in their religious beliefs and practices. They may be a national military threat. Why go to them?

> **Preface note:** At the time I taught this lesson in 2016, America's national enemies were the ISIS terrorists who had established a fortified base in Mosul, Iraq (the site of ancient Nineveh). Mosul was making front-page news, and Americans were sustaining casualties across the region. Videos clips had been aired, showing some of our own military troops—our sons and daughters—on their knees as terrorists prepared to behead them. National emotion was running very high at that moment against these terrorists. The Lord could not have blessed me with a more perfect example for this study of Jonah. Keep this context in mind as I work out the following parallel.

Sometimes we know about the people to whom we are being sent, but sometimes that knowledge is second-hand information. What do we really know about, say, the people of Iraq? ISIS is our enemy right now. Mosul, Iraq, is where the terrorists are based. We hear reports, see news clips, hear from people who have first-hand experience with them; but it is all second-hand information, and some of it is yesterday's news. Sometimes we build pictures and feelings about people but forget to allow for the possibility that circumstances may have changed, that they have changed from the people we think they are, and that God may be working in their lives.

We have our Ninevites in life, too.

Jonah has certain prejudices against Ninevites, but he also has an issue with God, which we discover in Jonah 4:2. After seeing the Ninevites repent, Jonah prays:

> *"... Ah, LORD, was not this what I said when I was still in my country? Therefore I fled previously to Tarshish; for I know that You are a gracious and merciful God, slow to anger and abundant in lovingkindness, One who relents from doing harm." Jonah 4:2*

His issue is that God is a gracious and merciful God. Who has *that* issue with God? Really?

The issue is not so much with God being merciful, but that He is being merciful to the Ninevites. We like it when God's gracious love and mercy extends to us, but it grates on us when it is extended to the Ninevites in our lives. We rationalize that there needs to be consequences for their wickedness, and mercy can come only after the consequences. Maybe.

What we must remember is that Jonah is an ambassador for God. When you are an ambassador, it is not about what you think or feel, or your personal assessment of the people, or how you weigh mercy and justice against them. You are there on God's behalf. The ambassador is supposed to take God's policy to the people, promote it, and live by it. When you are God's ambassador, it requires a certain amount of dying to self.

In Jonah's Shoes

Before we get too critical of Jonah, let's step into Jonah's shoes and consider what it might be like if God asks us to do the same thing. Consider this scenario:

> One day out of the blue, God tells one of us, "Arise, go to Mosul and cry out against it; for their wickedness has come up before Me."
>
> Mosul is a war-torn country at the moment. The local forces are trying to oust the terrorists and allied forces are rallying support. The war has brought famine and disease in the land. People are dying from lack of provision. In addition to the physical depravity, there is an overwhelming spiritual darkness in the land.
>
> An entire platoon of armed military men wouldn't venture in there at the moment, let alone a single Christian on foot, unarmed and without provision except what God gives him on the way, without physical reinforcement or protection, without possibility of rescue, and with a very unpopular message to deliver. Just getting there is a hike of some 560 miles as the crow flies from Israel's coast to Mosul (remember, this is on foot). When the Christian gets there, he must walk into the middle of the ISIS terrorist camp and tell them their wickedness has come up before our God, and He is getting ready to judge them.
>
> The physical mission itself is daunting, the message foolhardy, and we haven't even addressed how we feel about ISIS terrorists. What is our gut reaction toward them? Fear, loathing, hatred, contempt? When we see news clips of them beheading American soldiers, do we wish any mercy for the terrorists? When we hear of Christians being harassed and killed, of young Christian girls being raped and forced into Muslim harems, what kind of justice do we want to see? We feel about ISIS terrorists the way Jonah felt about Ninevites.

If one of us undertook Jonah's mission, what would the outcome be?

Would we be willing to die if we thought the Lord's wrath would fall on them?

Would we be willing to die if the Lord's wrath *wasn't* going to fall on them, but they would be granted mercy instead?

How many of us are in the same boat with Jonah?

Mercy

Jonah is called by God to be His ambassador on a particular mission and Jonah refuses, partly because of what he knows about Nineveh, but also because of what he knows about God. According to Jonah 4:2, it appears that Jonah's aversion to the mission is not so much a fear of death, but because he knows God will grant the Ninevites mercy if they repent. Jonah doesn't want God to show them mercy. He wants justice. I think mercy can be very hard to embrace because it implies an escape from consequences, and therefore, we think justice will not be served.

By sending Jonah to the Ninevites, God brings this issue of Jonah's lack of mercy to the surface. Jonah might think he is being sent to deal with the Ninevites' sin; in reality, the Ninevites are God's catalyst for dealing with Jonah's own lack of mercy.

A lack of mercy is a major character flaw in an ambassador for God. If you are an ambassador for God, you are a representative of God. People who don't know God should look at you and see God. Yet, there are aspects of God's character that we struggle with because of our own humanity, our own feelings, and our own limited understanding, which is what makes this a very tough job to do. Even so, the ambassador's job is to represent the King and promote the King's policy to the people of other countries. Mercy is one of those qualities of God's character that others should see in us.

What is mercy? By definition, mercy is showing compassion or forgiveness to someone you have the power to hurt or punish.

Think about the people in your own life for a moment. Who do you have the power to hurt, and who has the power to hurt you?

God gives us people in our lives over whom we have the power to hurt, and we have to decide how to balance justice with mercy in dealing with them. How do we weigh out mercy and justice? We often use a sliding scale, weighing out what we consider to be small and large offenses, and then punish or show mercy accordingly. Repeat offenses get the most severe punishment. We remember the past offenses and as those offenses add up, we weigh out more and more punishment and less and less mercy.

When the situation is reversed, though, and we are facing someone who has the power to hurt us or hand down our punishment, we want the scale to tilt more toward mercy for ourselves, don't we?

The Hebrew word for mercy is *chesed* (pronounced hesed) and carries a slightly different definition. In the Old Testament Scriptures, this word is translated most often as mercy, but also as kindness, goodness, and faithfulness. Each act of mercy on our part engages and develops those fruits of the Spirit. When the Lord sets out to develop those things in us, as He does here with Jonah, He is going to put us into a situation where we must choose to show mercy to someone. How we react in that situation is a test of how well we have developed those fruits of the Spirit in our lives.

God's Policy on Mercy

If we are going to be ambassadors for God, we should really know what is God's policy on justice and mercy. His policy is found in Ezekiel 18:20-29.

> *"The soul who sins shall die. The son shall not bear the guilt of the father, nor the father bear the guilt of the son. The righteousness of the righteous shall be upon himself, and the wickedness of the wicked shall be upon himself.*
>
> *But if a wicked man turns from all his sins which he has committed, keeps all My statutes, and does what is lawful and right, he shall surely live; he shall not die. None of the transgressions which he has committed shall be remembered against him; because of the righteousness which he has done, he shall live. Do I have any pleasure at all that the wicked should die?' says the Lord GOD, 'and not that he should turn from his ways and live?*
>
> *But when a righteous man turns away from his righteousness and commits iniquity, and does according to all the abominations that the wicked man does, shall he live? All the righteousness which he has done shall not be remembered; because of the unfaithfulness of which he is guilty and the sin which he has committed, because of them he shall die. Yet you say, 'The way of the Lord is not fair.' Hear now, O house of Israel, is it not My way which is fair, and your ways which are not fair?*
>
> *When a righteous man turns away from his righteousness, commits iniquity, and dies in it, it is because of the iniquity which he has done that he dies. Again, when a wicked man turns away from the wickedness which he committed, and does what is lawful and right, he preserves himself alive. Because he considers and turns away from all the transgressions which he committed, he shall surely live; he shall not die.*
>
> *Yet the house of Israel says, 'The way of the Lord is not fair.' O house of*

> Israel, is it not My ways which are fair, and your ways which are not fair?"
> —Ezekiel 18:20-29

"None of the transgressions which he has committed shall be remembered against him." A big part of mercy is letting go of the past, letting go of the history we have with people and the remembrance of offenses, even letting go of the emotions that the offense produced in us like anger, resentment, fear, or hurt. You really can't show mercy until you are willing to let go of all that. Forgiving is difficult, but forgetting is a much harder thing.

Keeping the Big Picture in View

God is a multi-tasker. Even as He is dealing with Jonah over the issue of mercy, He is also working out a bigger plan to deal with the nation of Israel as a whole. After sending Jonah to Nineveh, He sends Hosea and Amos to Israel, and Hosea's message, in particular, has the same focus on mercy. In Hosea 6:4-5, the Lord addresses both the northern kingdom of Israel (Ephraim) and the southern kingdom of Judah (Judah).

> *"O Ephraim, what shall I do to you? O Judah, what shall I do to you? For your faithfulness* [chesed] *is like a morning cloud, and like the early dew it goes away. Therefore I have hewn them by the prophets, I have slain them by the words of My mouth; and your judgments are like light that goes forth. For I desire mercy* [chesed] *and not sacrifice, and the knowledge of God more than burnt offerings."—Hosea 6:4-6*

Notice how, in this last verse, mercy and sacrifice appear on opposite ends of God's scale. Let's compare those.

The act of sacrifice takes a life—it's about paying the cost for sin. Man sins and his life is forfeit. In the Old Testament sacrificial system, as a substitute for the man's life, an animal's life is forfeit.

In contrast, the act of mercy saves a life. God says He would rather have a person live and not die. That is why His policy on mercy is the way it is.

The act of sacrifice represents a relationship with God based on obligation, and the sacrifice is a transaction on man's behalf, as covering for the sin. But like a transaction, it doesn't require engagement with God. According to the Law, if man breaks the law, then man must make the sacrifice and pay the restitution. Once that transaction is done, the man is good with God and goes back to his life. That sacrifice is just a transaction.

The act of mercy is different in this respect. It also represents a relationship with God, but it is not based on obligation, nor is it even about the man. The act of mercy is an act of intercession, sacrificing oneself on behalf of another. Where the transaction is merely between the man and God without thought to others, mercy is wholly focused on others.

In Hosea 4:6, mercy is paired with a knowledge of God. When the Lord begins to develop mercy in us, first He teaches us about His character, and then He extends mercy to us so that we see how it is modeled. Between the knowledge of God and the experience of His mercy, we should respond with a desire to be like Him . . . ideally.

Lessons in Mercy

God drives home a lesson of mercy for Jonah in the coming days. As He begins to work with Jonah, He takes him through the practice of mercy in stages.

First, God puts a group of sailors into Jonah's hands and gives Jonah the power to hurt them. Jonah has to make the decision whether or not to be merciful to them, and how to be merciful. These sailors are strangers to Jonah. They have none of the emotional associations that the Ninevites have, so it should be a simple decision on Jonah's part. God raises the stakes by adding the condition that if Jonah doesn't show mercy to them, the sailors will die.

After the lesson with the sailors, God turns the tables to make Jonah understand just how vulnerable he is. He takes Jonah into the belly of the fish and leaves him there until he begs for mercy for himself. If you do not show mercy for others, what right do you have to ask mercy for yourself?

The final lesson in Jonah 4 involves the death of a plant because of a worm. As a worm eats away at the plant and causes it to die, Jonah pities the plant and desires mercy on it (although his concern is less for the plant itself, and more over the impact its death has on his own comfort). The plant and the worm are small things whose life is fleeting. The Lord points out that Jonah has mercy for things of little importance but no mercy for things of great importance. The Lord ends the lesson with this *kal va'chomer*—light and heavy—illustration. If Jonah is merciful to a pathetic plant, how much more should he be toward people?

This is a lesson to keep in mind as we look at Jonah's story.

Confrontation and Avoidance

As ambassadors of God, we are often called to confront sinful behavior. Confrontation can be tough, especially when we are experiencing a very strong emotional reaction to the offender. Confrontation may be something we seek to avoid at all costs, like Jonah did. Jonah displays a number of avoidance behaviors: running away, hiding, and sleeping (a way of mentally disconnecting).

Maybe we avoid confrontation out of fear, hurt, prejudice, or because we feel it is not our place to say anything. Usually we confront people to whom we are close, with whom we have strong relationships or some level of authority, such as parent to child, husband to wife, boss to coworker, or friend to friend. Confronting someone often depends on how secure we feel with them and if we have some idea of how they will react (i.e., do they respect us, do they value our judgment, do they accept our authority?).

Avoiding the confrontation means the offense continues. Our anger and resentment continue to build, and we end up in a very dark place until the storm finally breaks, which it must, however much we avoid it. And the storm often gets worse the longer we avoid it. This is literally how the scenario is going to play out in Jonah's life.

Keep in mind, the Assyrians of Nineveh eventually become the conquerors of Israel. If you were Israel, would you rather be at the mercy of a nation who doesn't know God and has no respect for His people, or a nation who fears God? If you were Jonah, wouldn't you do whatever you could to get mercy for your people?

Jonah is called to a difficult mission and doesn't want to go. The Ninevites are brutal, pagan, and Israel's sworn enemies. Jonah's internal reaction to these people desires justice without mercy, much the same as we might feel toward terrorists. We want them dealt with, but we quail at a face-to-face confrontation because we are sure that the outcome will, with some certainty, end in our death. Worse yet than death, they might actually repent, the Lord may have mercy on them, and then we will have to forgive them and forget the atrocities they have done to us and our kinsmen.

Again, I ask, how many of us are in the boat with Jonah?

Applications

Are there people in your life who you just don't want to engage or share Christ with? If so, why?

In terms of mercy, who do you have the power to hurt or punish?

How do you personally weigh mercy and punishment for those people in your life?

How good are you at letting go of past offenses?

To whom are you vulnerable? Who has the power to hurt you?

Have you ever experienced mercy from others in your life? If so, when?

What are the benefits of God's policy on mercy?

Why is confrontation necessary at times?

Have you ever confronted a perfect stranger over sinful behavior?

Have you ever avoided confronting someone? Why?

What did Jonah do to avoid confrontation?

What strategies do you use?

What are some consequences of avoiding confrontation?

Does avoiding a person make the problem better or worse in the long run?

Who do you think Jonah's avoidance will benefit the most?

Is avoidance an others-focused or self-focused behavior?

God is going to put Jonah through two lessons in mercy—one in which he has the power to give or withhold mercy, and one in which he is powerless and must ask for mercy.

Which lesson do you think will be easier? Why?

Which lesson would it take to make you a more merciful person?

Jonah 1: Jonah and the Sailors

FROM THE SAILORS' PERSPECTIVE

> *"But Jonah arose to flee to Tarshish from the presence of the LORD. He went down to Joppa, and found a ship going to Tarshish; so he paid the fare, and went down into it, to go with them to Tarshish from the presence of the LORD. But the LORD sent out a great wind on the sea, and there was a mighty tempest on the sea, so that the ship was about to be broken up. Then the mariners were afraid; and every man cried out to his god, and threw the cargo that was in the ship into the sea, to lighten the load. But Jonah had gone down into the lowest parts of the ship, had lain down, and was fast asleep."*
> —Jonah 1:3-5

For this lesson, let's look at the events of this passage from the point of view of the sailors, which I think is an important perspective. When we, as ambassadors of God, begin down the path of disobedience, the people around us see that. They see God's hand on us for better or worse, and they also suffer the storm our disobedience brings into their lives. If we could see our behavior through other people's eyes and the negative impact we have on them, it might break our self-centered focus and help us regain some perspective. It might even spur us to change our behavior, if only for their sakes. Maybe.

Today we will stand with the sailors of the ships of Tarshish. We will pretend we know nothing about Jonah and his God, Jehovah, Who we have not met yet. Jonah is a stranger to us. We come in contact with strangers every day without knowing anything about their lives, their circumstances, their beliefs, or their struggles, and they don't know ours. For a moment in time, we are thrown together with this stranger under a certain set of circumstances that quickly develop into a crisis situation. We watch how he responds to the crisis, what he does or doesn't do, what he says or doesn't say, and we try to get a sense of who he is. His actions and reactions surprise us, even appall us. He brings a storm into our lives that isn't of our making, but we end up having to make some very difficult decisions to deal with his problem.

When God brings people into our lives, there is a lesson that works both ways. We may think we are dealing with their problems, when in fact they are the catalyst to expose our condition and test our character. Even as God deals with Jonah, He also tests the mercy of the sailors.

Getting into Character

Who are the sailors of the ships of Tarshish?

> "... For the king's ships went to Tarshish with the servants of Hiram. Once every three years the merchant ships came, bringing gold, silver, ivory, apes, and monkeys."—2 Chronicles 9:20-21

> [Speaking to the city of Tyre] *"Tarshish was your merchant because of your many luxury goods. They gave you silver, iron, tin, and lead for your goods. . . . The ships of Tarshish were carriers of your merchandise. You were filled and very glorious in the midst of the seas. Your oarsmen brought you into many waters, but the east wind broke you in the midst of the seas."*—Ezekiel 27:12, 25-26

During his reign, Solomon engaged Hiram of Tyre and the ships of Tarshish to import gold and luxury items for the Temple and Solomon's many other building projects. It became a very lucrative business arrangement, continuing through the many generations of Israel's kings. Once every three years, the ships of Tarshish put into port at Joppa in Israel to pick up merchandise and occasionally passengers.

In this exercise, we are the sailors responsible for a very precious cargo—metals, precious gems, exotic spices, slaves, livestock and horses, Egyptian linen, African ivory and ebony, and all forms of commodities. The kings of Israel will use the ships of Tarshish to trade their wheat, honey, oil, and balm.

A lot rides on our getting this precious cargo to port, since it is our livelihood and several years' worth of income for us and our families back home. It is the livelihood of our investors. If something happens to our cargo on the journey, the fortune of many lives is at stake.

We come from all over the Mediterranean, a mixture of nationalities and pagan beliefs. Each sailor has his own god. We may have heard about the God of Israel, but we don't know Him or believe in Him. What we know of our gods is that they are changeable and moody, rarely benevolent, easily angered, generally unmerciful, and only placated with sacrifices.

We have been sailing a long time, and we can tell stories of some of the storms we have encountered in our travels. The worst of these storms always comes from the east, out of the Arabian Desert. When the hot east wind blowing off the desert hits the cooler Mediterranean coast, it creates something like a tropical storm. These storms cross over the Mediterranean and cause severe weather at sea. Ships with heavy cargos like ours are particularly at risk of going down in these kind of seas and we fear them, as Israel's King David wrote in his Psalms,

> *"Fear took hold of them there, and pain, as of a woman in birth pangs, as when You break the ships of Tarshish with an east wind." —Psalms 48:6-7*

When the east wind blows, it is something to be greatly feared.

But today is a beautiful Mediterranean day. We put into port at Joppa, and are busy loading cargo into the ship. A stranger pays for passage to Tarshish and comes aboard. He disappears below deck, and we don't think any more about him as we prepare to depart.

We set sail with clear skies and fair sailing, loaded with precious cargo and a stranger. We haven't gotten far from Israel, maybe a few days' sailing, when the east wind picks up. All sailors of the ships of Tarshish know the east wind is an ill omen.

The New King James Version says the Lord sent out a mighty wind, but the Hebrew is much more descriptive. It says God "hurled down" a storm. Very quickly the wind strengthens and continues growing in speed and intensity. We become very afraid.

The Storm

As the storm breaks over us, we do two things. We cry out to our gods, and we throw things into the sea. It's interesting that we immediately interpret this storm as an act of divine wrath, but that is what our beliefs teach us these things mean. To appease our gods, we throw things into the sea "to lighten the load." This isn't about lightening the weight of the ship so that it will stay afloat. In the Hebrew, the phrase "to lighten the load" means to lighten the divine punishment that is coming on you by putting away something that is cursed. We believe that somehow, inadvertently, we brought something cursed on board, and that is what brought this storm of divine wrath on us.

Our gods are not like Israel's God. They don't tell us where the problem is. They don't tell us why they are angry at us. We have to guess. So we start throwing precious cargo overboard, trying to rid ourselves of the one cursed thing, whatever it is. One thing goes overboard, yet the storm rages. It wasn't that. Another item goes overboard, yet the storm rages. It wasn't that either. As we work our way down through the ship, into the ship hold, finally in the lowest part of the boat, we find the stranger. Down there, in the midst of our luxury goods, this stranger made a bed for himself with our Egyptian cotton and linen sheets, and he is snoring away. The Hebrew word for sleep used here means to snore noisily.

The storm is raging, the ship is being tossed around, the crew is alarmed and in an uproar, yet this man is sleeping as if he hasn't a care in the world. There is something very wrong with his behavior.

The Confrontation

Our captain is at wits' end, trying to figure out what is wrong and how to save the ship, and here is this stranger sleeping away, completely out of touch and out of sync with everyone else. If you were the captain, how much effort would you take in this moment of crisis to deal with this person? Not much. Our frustrated captain wastes only a moment of time in confronting this man.

> *"So the captain came to him, and said to him, 'What do you mean, sleeper? Arise, call on your God; perhaps your God will consider us, so that we may not perish.'"—Jonah 1:6*

In a perfectly natural response, our captain shakes him and exclaims, "You need to wake up to what is going on around you! Get up! Get moving! Find a way to help! All of us have been calling on our gods to no avail. Maybe it's not our gods that are angry. Maybe it's *your* God. Perhaps if you call on your God, He will be merciful to us and keep us from perishing!

How does the stranger respond? He doesn't. There is no response from Jonah recorded in the passage in this moment. How a person responds or doesn't respond can tell us a lot about their character.

This is the initial confrontation. There has to be a confrontation, because when we see this kind of odd behavior, we must say something to this man, but we aren't going to waste a lot of time on him. We're still throwing things overboard, trying to rid ourselves of the accursed thing that has caused someone's God to storm at us. But nothing is working.

When we have thrown everything overboard, then what? It occurs to us that maybe it's not something on our ship but somebody. Maybe somebody on this ship is in trouble with his God and doesn't want to own up to it. Surely, someone on this ship knows something. The only way to figure this out is the age-old method of divine determination—the casting of lots.

> *"And they said to one another, 'Come, let us cast lots, that we may know for whose cause this trouble has come upon us.' So they cast lots, and the lot fell on Jonah. Then they said to him, 'Please tell us! For whose cause is*

this trouble upon us? What is your occupation? And where do you come from? What is your country? And of what people are you?'" —Jonah 1:7-8

The Lord helps us a little by nudging the lots so they point to the sleepy passenger. We had passed over him before and had been ignoring him all this time, but now he has our full attention. We know that he knows something, and we start peppering him with questions.

"For whose cause has this trouble come upon us?" We haven't quite connected with the fact that he *is* the problem. We just think he knows something, and maybe we expect him to point his finger at one of us. We haven't been thinking about him. We have only been looking at ourselves, thinking we were the ones who brought on this storm.

I want to pause in the narrative for a moment to sketch a quick outline of a character type that Jonah is modeling for us. I think God brings these kinds of people into our lives at times to test our understanding of mercy.

Jonah as a Type

From what we have seen of Jonah so far, in what he has done or not done, said or not said, we can see some characteristics emerging that are similar to people we run into in our lives today. The Jonah character is not a person who is great on taking responsibility in life—not for himself and, most certainly, not for others. He (or she) is oblivious to what is going on in the real world, being very much immersed in his own little drama. His life has become a series of peaks and valleys into which he will gladly drag us if we let him. He expects our support in his crisis; but when the crisis is in our lives, he is no help at all.

We find Jonahs like this in our lives, and we don't always know how they got there. They just show up; and before we know it, they have made a comfortable little nest for themselves in our lives, maybe even in our homes, and are taking advantage of all the benefits and good things that a relationship with us brings. They don't contribute. They don't communicate. As a result, they grate on everyone. Without lifting a finger, Jonah is already grating on the captain and crew here in the narrative.

Another thing about Jonahs is that they bring a storm into our lives and yet have a way of making everyone else feel that the storm is their own fault. They relieve themselves of that responsibility by placing it on others.

This is the kind of character with whom the sailors are now having to deal. Now, back to our narrative.

The Confession

The lots have been cast, and they point to the stranger. Having been put on the spot, he finally speaks a few brief words.

> *"So he said to them, 'I am a Hebrew; and I fear the LORD, the God of heaven, who made the sea and the dry land.' Then the men were exceedingly afraid, and said to him, 'Why have you done this?' For the men knew that he fled from the presence of the LORD, because he had told them."*—Jonah 1:9-10

He is one of *them*. He's one of those Israelites. We have heard about them, and we've heard about their God.

We should note how the stranger introduces his God here. He calls Him the *"God of heaven, who made the sea and the dry land."* Now we, the pagan sailors, may worship the god of the sea, or any number of gods of the natural world, but the way the stranger describes his God trumps all in the hierarchy of gods. He serves the Creator God. If His God is in the heaven *and* the sea *and* the land, where can you go to get away from Him? Nowhere.

We, the sailors, hear this and become very afraid when the stranger finally identifies himself. To give you an idea of the kind of fear we are feeling, I am going to paint you a modern day scenario.

> It is a beautiful September day, the year 2001, and we go to work in our office in one of the twin towers of the World Trade Center. All of a sudden, we feel an impact, and the building shudders. A plane has crashed into it. The building sways and begins to crumble. A firestorm breaks out, smoke fills the rooms, and debris falls all around us. Panic sets in, and people run around, looking for an escape.

> In that moment of panic, as we pass the employee lounge, we see a man sitting there, just sitting there, drinking a cup of coffee. Maybe he has some earphones on. Maybe he's flipping through a magazine. But he isn't panicking. He isn't trying to escape. He isn't trying to help people. He isn't doing anything. He is just sitting there. So we go shake him, and scream, "Get up! Why aren't you doing something?" And he just looks at us and simply says, "I am a Muslim. I serve Allah. Allah akbar."

Those few words with which he identifies himself—who he is and who he serves—speak volumes to us. His odd behavior, the fact that he doesn't feel the need to save his own life, and the firestorm raining down on our heads all come together at once in our understanding, and bring a horror on us that is indescribable. That is the kind of horror Jonah's words have inspired in the sailors.

The Story

We, the sailors, don't know this man's God, and don't believe in his God. But *he* believes in his God. He tells us that he has run away from his God, and his God has come for him.

The passage doesn't elaborate as to how Jonah explains his actions to the sailors, but please allow me to speculate a little based on what I know personally from a Jonah who came into my life.

When you confront a Jonah in your life as the sailors do here, what you get is a story. Remember, a Jonah is a self-centered person but also a self-promoting person. He (or she, in my case) spins you a story that is part truth, but may not be the whole story. It may go something like this:

> "I was in a bad relationship and I need to get away for a while . . . I was in a partnership with a person who wanted me to do something I just didn't feel right doing . . . I need to get a clean start . . . I have some medical problems so I can't work anymore. Now I'm unemployed and need help buying medicine."

This is how my personal Jonah's story went. And almost immediately she began to make a nest in my life. She wanted to use my phone and my address to get her social security checks. She ate my food, and watched my TV. It didn't take her any time at all to get comfortable. She stayed one night and the next morning, when I knocked on the bedroom door to tell her I was going to work, I was rebuffed for interrupting her while she was praying.

There was something odd in her behavior that bothered me, and when I saw her beginning to make a nest, I pushed her along into another living situation. This woman had a storm in her life that would have come into my life if I had let it go on any further.

I have seen other people who have let the Jonahs in their life stay. What they eventually found out the hard way was that Jonahs don't make good decisions and are (usually) in rebellion to some authority. Inevitably, these authorities end up on the person's doorstep looking for the Jonah. These Jonahs usually have debts they cannot pay or are trying to avoid paying (another story), and so debt collectors begin to call. Jonahs bring these kinds of issues into a person's life, and suddenly those issues are then the problem with which the other person has to deal.

It all begins with a story that is slanted to appeal to our mercy, so that we have pity on them. We should recognize in this moment that even as God is dealing with this Jonah and his issues, He is testing our mercy as well. He wants to see a little bit of His own character in us. So God lets the narrative play out in our lives to see how we balance mercy with justice toward someone completely undeserving—how much kindness, how much goodness, and how much faithfulness we show in sticking with this person, and at what point we cut them off.

The Solution

Having heard Jonah's story, we, the sailors, ask why. Why have you done this? We see the poor decisions that have been made. We see through the story. Another question follows the first.

> *"Then they said to him, 'What shall we do to you that the sea may be calm for us?'—for the sea was growing more tempestuous."—Jonah 1:11*

What shall we do to *you* that the sea may become calm for *us*? Jonah just hit a wall with us, and now we distance ourselves from him. We put up some resistance because of how we perceive his actions, and sides are drawn between him and us. We understand very clearly that this is Jonah's issue with his God. It has nothing to do with us, and we want out. So you, Jonah, give us the solution and tell us what needs to be done at this point.

> *"And he said to them, 'Pick me up and throw me into the sea; then the sea will become calm for you. For I know that this great tempest is because of me.'"—Jonah 1:12*

We have to remember through all this that Jonah is, after all, a prophet of God, and God speaks through him. But if you don't know who he is as a prophet or about his God, you might take his statement as a little over-dramatic. "Just throw me into the sea, and your troubles will be over"—as if we would do that. We are good people, kind people, merciful people. We don't just throw people into the sea when we know it will kill them. We are not murderers. And so we grapple with what to do with this Jonah on our ship, and rationalize a little. What has he really done to us to deserve a death penalty (besides causing us to lose our cargo)? Even so, he has this issue with his God, and we need to get out of the middle of it. What will his God do to us if we interfere? Will it go against us?

In a modern-day context, we also grapple over what to do with the Jonahs in our lives, and we rationalize. Maybe we say to ourselves, "At least when they are in our house, we can be a good example . . . maybe we can get them to go to church . . . maybe we can get them to read their Bible and talk to God . . . maybe our good example will spur them to be a better person and get their life back on track." We make these kinds of rationalizations.

That being said, somewhere in the back of our minds, some other questions might be hovering. If he knows he is the problem, why doesn't he take the necessary steps to deal with the problem? Why doesn't he throw himself over? Why make us responsible for his death? Why make us feel as if we are abandoning him?

This is another form of their manipulation. The Jonahs in life push off the responsibility, make it our problem, and then make us feel guilty when hard decisions have to be made to deal with their problem. They make us feel like we are abandoning them when we try to distance ourselves from the storm they have caused.

This stranger is not being very merciful to us. He could have pleaded with his God to have mercy on us, but he didn't. He could have thrown himself over and spared us the guilt. He's certainly not being as merciful to us as we are to him.

Yet we keep rowing.

> *"Nevertheless the men rowed hard to return to land, but they could not, for the sea continued to grow more tempestuous against them."—Jonah 1:13*

The nearest land is Israel, so that is where we try to go. Does Jonah want to return to Israel? No. Jonah isn't helping. Even when you try to save them, to drag them back in the direction their life ought to go, Jonahs tend to be self-sabotaging. In addition to that, the storm blows us away from Israel. God isn't helping either. He decides to keep us all out in deep water.

Why do we continue to row until we are at our physicals limit? We do this for all those reasons we rationalize about—being merciful people, being a good influence, and helping them get their life turned around and back to God. Yet for all of our good intentions, we must at some point come to the conclusion that our merciful example isn't having any effect.

We need to understand that God must take Jonah to the next level of the lesson, which is going to be just between Jonah and God. God cannot do this until we let go. There comes a point where we have to let Jonah go so that God can deal one-on-one with him and accomplish the breaking that is needed to make him useful again to His plan. God casts us in that merciful savior persona for a brief while, partly for our sake so that we might have an opportunity to exercise the kindness, goodness, faithfulness, and mercy that are aspects of His character. But we have to keep in perspective who we are and who God is. God is working in this person's life, and there comes a time when our efforts can get in the way. We are not necessarily abandoning our Jonahs when we abandon them to God.

The Resolution

We, the sailors, finally make a decision to wash our hands of Jonah. Before we commit him to the deep, we pray this prayer to Jonah's God:

> *"Therefore they cried out to the LORD and said, 'We pray, O LORD, please do not let us perish for this man's life, and do not charge us with innocent blood; for You, O LORD, have done as it pleased You.' So they picked up Jonah and threw him into the sea, and the sea ceased from its raging."—Jonah 1:14-15*

We have received no mercy from the man, yet we appeal to his God for mercy. "Please do not let us perish for this man's life . . ." This issue is between God and His servant. Having done some self-searching, we ask not to be charged with a sin against innocent blood as it appears we have been given no choice concerning this man. We acknowledge that this Creator God is sovereign and in control of the events unfolding here.

Then we pick Jonah up and toss him overboard. A moment later, the wind dies down and the sea becomes calm. Just as quickly as the storm spun up, it dissipates, leaving only the sloshing of waves against the boat.

What have we just learned?

Jonah said if we threw him into the sea, it would be calm for us—and it happened. So he really was a prophet and what he said was true. If that was true, what else did he say? He said his God was the God of heaven, Who made the sea and dry land. That must be true, too. And if He is this powerful—and merciful—and He works this way in our lives, what kind of relationship should we have with Him?

> *"Then the men feared the LORD exceedingly, and offered a sacrifice to the LORD and took vows."—Jonah 1:16*

We, as heathen, have no idea how to worship this God, but we do what is in our hearts to do. Apparently this God accepts us since there aren't any further repercussions for having thrown His prophet overboard.

What happens to us after this? The storm is over, the sea is calm, we have no cargo, and we are in need of repairs. We need to get to a port somewhere. When we get to that port, people look at our ship and ask "What happened to you?" And we tell them about the storm and about Jonah and about this encounter with the God of heaven and earth. And our story then spreads from port to port, as another prophet of God foretold:

> *"I will set a sign among them; and those among them who escape I will*

send to the nations: to Tarshish and Pul and Lud, who draw the bow, and Tubal and Javan, to the coastlands afar off who have not heard My fame nor seen My glory. And they shall declare My glory among the Gentiles."
—Isaiah 66:19

The Lord always leaves survivors for His purpose.

And to think, King David, so many generations earlier, prophesied of just this story.

"Those who go down to the sea in ships, who do business on great waters, they see the works of the LORD, and His wonders in the deep. For He commands and raises the stormy wind, which lifts up the waves of the sea. They mount up to the heavens, they go down again to the depths; Their soul melts because of trouble. They reel to and fro, and stagger like a drunken man, and are at their wits' end. Then they cry out to the LORD in their trouble, and He brings them out of their distresses. He calms the storm, so that its waves are still. Then they are glad because they are quiet; so He guides them to their desired haven. Oh, that men would give thanks to the LORD for His goodness, and for His wonderful works to the children of men! Let them exalt Him also in the assembly of the people, and praise Him in the company of the elders."—Psalm 107:23-32

Application

Have you ever encountered someone who appealed to your mercy, even though you knew this person was just using you? If so, how did you react to them?

What are some characteristic warning signs that tell us we are dealing with a Jonah in our life?

Why would you keep rowing for your Jonah or for how long?

Reflecting back, did God use that person in your life to teach you something about yourself? If so, how?

This is the end of the first chapter, studied from the point of view of the sailors. Through the sailors' eyes, Jonah becomes a type of character we meet in life. He is a person God brings into our life to test how well we are developing mercy in our character. As we struggle to show mercy to our Jonahs, we should be reminded of God's mercy toward us when we were just as undeserving. Even so, there comes a point when we realize it is time to step out of the picture and let God deal with Jonah.

Now let's go back through the same chapter from Jonah's perspective.

Jonah 1: Jonah and the Sailors (Revisited)

FROM JONAH'S PERSPECTIVE

Getting into Character

As we step into Jonah's character, and look at the same events from his perspective, let's ask ourselves a few questions.

Are there times in our lives when:

- We fall short of modeling the Lord's example of love, forgiveness, patience, self-control, etc.?
- The sheer revulsion we feel over particular sins in people's lives keeps us from engaging them?
- We struggle with something spiritually and are just not focused on others?
- We are jolted awake by someone's reaction to us?
- We know the truth of something but keep our mouth shut?
- We could have told someone the truth and saved them a lot of heartache?
- We could have done something to remedy a bad situation but didn't?
- We are given the perfect opportunity to witness for God but don't take it?

We have all been in the same boat as Jonah.

For this exercise, we are Jonah. We are God's prophet, which means we agree to act as God's ambassador, even when it means confronting wickedness in our world. The Lord tells us to go to a particular heathen people and deliver a warning, but we don't want to do it. We know that if we deliver this message and the people repent, God will have mercy on them and stay His judgment because He is a merciful God.

But they are Ninevites—heathen enemies. This is a sticking point for us. We are so repulsed by their sinful heathen lifestyle, pagan beliefs, and past offenses that we don't think they deserve mercy. We want wrath to fall on them. So we refuse this particular mission.

God's Lesson Plan

When we, standing in Jonah's shoes, choose to get on the boat to Tarshish instead of heading for Nineveh, not only are we choosing not to help the Ninevites, but we are also rebelling against God. Our actions say to Him, "No, we are not going to do this, *and You can't make us*." We challenge the Lord's sovereignty and authority over our lives. This now escalates to a much bigger issue between us and God, and God is going to have to re-establish Who He is and who we are in our understanding. God has already engaged us in a lesson of mercy, but now He expands that lesson to accomplish the following objectives:

1. To give us a taste of what it is like to be out of His presence, and to realize the pleasures of this world are fleeting
2. To show us that our disobedience has made us little better than the heathen we despise
3. To get our acknowledgement of who we are and Who He is
4. To teach us to desire mercy and show mercy to others, if only for our own sake

We begin a downward journey into disobedience and rebellion. We go down to Joppa, and now down into the ship (Jonah 1:3). Before we finish, we will go down into the belly of the great fish, and finally down into the depths of the sea. Down, down, down, down. Here, at the mid-point of that downward journey, God begins a dialogue with us in the form of a storm and gives us the opportunity to repent and return to Him. We have two options: turn back or continue downward.

From the sailors' eyes, we appear to be self-focused and self-serving, wrapped up in our own little world; and they are right because that is what rebellion and disobedience do to us. They turn our focus inward on ourselves and make us blind to the impact our actions have on the people around us. In keeping with that character, we aren't going to care what the sailors think of us or be overly concerned with them because we are wrapped up in this all-consuming conflict with God.

We keep telling ourselves that:

> We don't want to think about God.
> We don't want to talk about God.
> We left God back in Israel.
> We have no God.

We say these things to ourselves, but we know we are deceiving ourselves. Just because we aren't acknowledging God in this moment doesn't mean He isn't there. We *do* have a God and He pursues us with great patience and persistence. He is right here with us in the storm, and in spite of our lack of submission, He wants to use us for His purpose.

Fleeing from the Presence of the Lord

Here is the folly of disobedience. In order to avoid going to a heathen country to offer mercy to the heathen, we choose to board a ship full of heathen bound for a heathen country. This is just the kind of foolish thing we find ourselves doing when we rebel against God's will in our lives. The fact is, we are so busy running away and looking over our shoulder at what's behind us, that we don't look where we are going, trip ourselves up, and get into these messes. At times like this, I think God laughs at us, but then turns it into a lesson. We don't want to be an ambassador to heathen Ninevites? Fine. He makes us an ambassador to heathen sailors. It is good practice after all, and God doesn't waste any experience.

If we think clearly in this moment and don't just react blindly to what God asks us to do, logic and reasoning present a few points to consider:

1) Can we really get away from God? We see in the next chapter that although we, Jonah, know the Psalms very well, this particular psalm is pointedly ignored.

   "Where can I go from Your Spirit? Or where can I flee from Your presence? If I ascend into heaven, You are there; if I make my bed in hell, behold, You are there. If I take the wings of the morning, and dwell in the uttermost parts of the sea, even there Your hand shall lead me, and Your right hand shall hold me. If I say, 'Surely the darkness shall fall on me,' even the night shall be light about me; indeed, the darkness shall not hide from You, but the night shines as the day; the darkness and the light are both alike to You."—Psalm 139:7-12

2) What do we think life is like away from the presence of the Lord? Are we even thinking of the benefits we stand to lose? The Scripture teaches us that God is a source of these things: light, rest, provision, peace, refuge (escape), strength, and life. When we leave God behind, do we leave behind these things as well?

3) When we find a new source for these things that replaces or rivals God in our lives, isn't that, by definition, idolatry? An idol is something that

becomes our substitute for God. So, our rebellion takes us down the path to idolatry.

We are Jonah, a Hebrew man living in Old Testament times, which means we are under the Law. We know from the Law which blessings go with obedience and which curses go with disobedience.

> *"And it shall be, that just as the LORD rejoiced over you to do you good and multiply you, so the LORD will rejoice over you to destroy you and bring you to nothing; and you shall be plucked from off the land which you go to possess. Then the LORD will scatter you among all peoples, from one end of the earth to the other, and there you shall serve other gods, which neither you nor your fathers have known—wood and stone. And among those nations you shall find no rest, nor shall the sole of your foot have a resting place; but there the LORD will give you a trembling heart, failing eyes, and anguish of soul. Your life shall hang in doubt before you; you shall fear day and night, and have no assurance of life. In the morning you shall say, 'Oh, that it were evening!' And at evening you shall say, 'Oh, that it were morning!' because of the fear which terrifies your heart, and because of the sight which your eyes see."—Deuteronomy 28:63-67*

We know all this, but we conveniently forget Scriptures like this because...

> We don't want to think about God.
> We don't want to talk to God.
> We left God in Israel.
> We have no God ... and now we have started down the path to idolatry.

The Lull before the Storm

We should note there is a lull before the storm (Jonah 1:3).

We went down to Joppa. God didn't stop us.

We paid our fare on the boat. God didn't stop us.

We went down into the lowest part of the boat and found a world full of treasures in the cargo of that ship. They are not our treasures, but they represent the promises of all the world can offer. Very quickly we get in bed with a new worldly lifestyle that is really only a dream. It's a little dark down in this hold ... but then it is easier to dream in the dark.

This is the lull before the storm.

We are lulled into a false sense of security.

We are lulled into the promise of wealth and luxury—the dream.

We are lulled into believing in our own strength—that we can do this on our own.

The Confrontation

> *"So the captain came to him, and said to him, 'What do you mean, sleeper? Arise, call on your God; perhaps your God will consider us, so that we may not perish.'"—Jonah 1:6*

As we are dreaming away, we are rudely awakened by the captain shaking us. He seems irritated and frustrated with us for some reason. We don't know what his problem is because we have been down here out of the way, minding our own business this whole time. He shouts commands at us.

"Wake Up!" the captain thunders. Why? Because disaster is upon us. There is a storm, and it is breaking up the ship.

(If a complete stranger ever says to us something along the lines of "When are you going to wake up . . .," it should be a red flag that something is very wrong in our lives.)

We wake up, but then we *really* wake up. We feel the storm wrecking the ship, but the storm outside is nothing compared to the storm now raging inside us *because we know.* We know it is God doing this, and it's because of us. We thought it would be easy to walk away from God. We didn't count on Him pursuing us. We thought He would just let us go, and we would be free. But we made a covenant with Him, and we haven't fulfilled our part of the bargain. We owe Him, and now He is coming to collect.

>We don't want to think about God.
>We don't want to talk about God.
>We left God back in Israel . . .

"Get up!" the captain shouts. Why? Because they think something on board is cursed so everything is getting tossed overboard, including that beautiful nest we made for ourselves. We just got comfortable, and the hold is being emptied before our eyes.

We watch these heathen throw all the pleasant things of life overboard. All the gold and gems and precious metals. All the fine linen and cotton. The wheat and oil and honey and balm. That's someone's investment. That's someone's security. That's our dream. All are gone in a moment. How fleeting are the pleasures of this world . . .

We watch, and we think what a waste it is to sacrifice all this to appease a nonexistent god. We know there is only one God (Yahweh Elohim) and there aren't any other gods. Sacrificing all this stuff to their gods isn't going to do them a lick of good, because *there are no other gods*. We know the mercy they are looking for will never come, and they will lose their lives. They are only hurting themselves.

But we don't tell them that. We keep our mouths shut. They get no mercy from us.

Our world just changed. All pleasures and comforts have been thrown into the sea. There is nowhere to sit, nowhere to lie down, no comfort or pleasure, no more rest or peace, no provisions left, nowhere to go, and no way to escape. There is nothing left. Our security is gone. The following things have now gone out of our lives: rest, provision, peace, refuge (escape), and strength. We don't even have much light left.

We want to be out of God's presence, and now we taste the bitterness of what life is really going to be like without Him, and it isn't pleasant.

God's Objective #1 accomplished: Let us taste what it is like to be out of His presence.

When we see the sailors pitching their cargo into the sea, why don't we say something to stop the senseless sacrifice?

> We don't want to think about God.
> We don't want to talk to God . . .

"**Pray to your God!**" the captain pleads. Why? Because maybe He will have mercy on us!

Why do these sailors talk to us like we are one of them? We are not just another Gentile appealing to a powerless idol. We are a prophet serving Yahweh Elohim. These people are heathens—no better than the Ninevites. We despise heathens. Why should we ask God to have mercy on them?

Because we are in the same boat with them.

We tell ourselves that we left God back in Israel. We have no God. By walking away from God we have become one of them. We have become no better than heathens. We have become what we despised.

God's Objective #2 accomplished: Our disobedience makes us no better than the heathen.

If the storm is breaking only in *our* lives, then we might ride it out and take the consequences. But the Lord raised the stakes by putting other lives at risk. He put their lives in our hands, and we now have the power to help them or hurt them. So He is forcing the issue of mercy in our lives.

Yes, they are heathen, but they haven't done us any harm, and we have no grievance against them. They beg us to call on our God and ask Him to spare them. From what we know of the Lord, He is merciful and will do this. But to save them, we must speak to God.

What do we do? We keep our mouths shut. We aren't talking to God.

What is it going to cost us if we speak up? Nothing but our pride.

What would happen if we prayed to God at this moment, and everyone was saved?

Up to this point, the sailors think this is just a freak storm—and maybe there is something on the ship that is cursed. They haven't realized yet that we are the cause. What would happen if we prayed to God now? Maybe God would stop the storm. Maybe these simple sailors would praise us and our God, and go on their way without stopping to question what caused the storm in the first place. We could just keep this issue between ourselves and God, with no one the wiser. But we aren't speaking to God. We make Him drag it out of us, and, as a result, the consequences are worse for us.

Have you ever given someone the silent treatment? Is there a point when you feel foolish for doing so—that it is no longer working to your advantage?

Meanwhile, the sailors cast lots.

Immediately, we know we are done for because we know this is one of God's favorite ways of revealing the sins we try to hide. God will tell them we are the culprit. All He has to do is flip that lot in our favor, and then they will all know. No, no, no . . . *rats*!

The moment for saving face is gone. The lot fell to us. The entire crew turns and looks at us. They have yet to realize that we are the problem, but they know we know something about this storm, so, they begin peppering us with questions (Jonah 1:8):

> *"Then they said to him, 'Please tell us! For whose cause is this trouble upon us? What is your occupation? And where do you come from? What is your country? And of what people are you?'"—Jonah 1:8*

The Confession

We can almost hear God chuckling. Go ahead, Jonah, tell them *who you are* and *Who I am*. They are waiting.

They put us on the spot, and now we have to acknowledge Who God is and who we are, publically, in front of the whole crew of heathen sailors.

> "So he said to them, 'I am a Hebrew; and I fear the LORD, the God of heaven, who made the sea and the dry land.'"—Jonah 1:9

God's Objective #3 accomplished: Get us to acknowledge who we are and Who He is.

God brings us to a point of submission and re-establishes Who He is in our lives. We acknowledge Him publically. It's been embarrassing and humbling, but our ordeal is not over yet because the sailors want an explanation. God wants to hear our explanation as well. What do we confess?

If we tell them the bald truth of why the storm is happening, what do we say?

The bald truth of why we ended up on this boat is that we despise heathens in general, and Ninevites in particular. We think they are brutal, ignorant, offensive, unworthy of mercy, and wish God's wrath would fall on the whole lot of them.

Do you really want to explain all this to a group of heathen sailors when you are stuck on a boat with them and just cost them their cargo, and maybe even their lives?

Here is another issue. When we wrestle with a spiritual issue in our relationship with God, people see it. Our disobedience makes our behavior look odd. It doesn't make sense to them, but they want to make sense of it. So they ask us, what is going on with you? Why are you acting this way?

How do we explain our spiritual wrestling with our God to a people who don't know our God?

They don't know anything about living as a child of God. They don't have our ethics or our morals. If we tell them, they look at us like we're nuts. How much do we explain? This is a dilemma for us, and it is a dilemma that our disobedience has caused.

So now we are on trial and stand condemned.

- We are obviously cursed, just as the Lord said we would be in Deuteronomy 28.
- We have been driven from Israel to a heathen nation by our disobedience.
- We have become an astonishment, a proverb, and a byword in the nations where we are being driven (Deuteronomy 28:37).
- We have already taken a step into idolatry in our pursuit of worldly riches—all of which disappeared in a moment, like a vapor.
- We have no rest, peace, refuge, or escape.
- And now, our very life hangs in doubt, and we have no assurance of life (Deuteronomy 28:66).
- We have come to the point where our persistent disobedience is driving people away from us. They aren't reasoning with us anymore, and they aren't showing much concern for us.

But if we return to the Lord, He promise to take us back and have compassion on us. So we face the following choice:

> *"See, I have set before you today life and good, death and evil, . . . I call heaven and earth as witnesses today against you, that I have set before you life and death, blessing and cursing; therefore choose life, that both you and your descendants may live; that you may love the LORD your God, that you may obey His voice, and that you may cling to Him, for He is your life and the length of your days; and that you may dwell in the land . . ."*
> —Deuteronomy 30:15, 19-20

Return to me, God whispers to us. There is still time to put an end to this storm. One simple prayer, one act of submission, and this whole ordeal could be over. But think for a minute of the consequences for us if we speak up at this point.

1) The sea becomes calm. We lose the cargo but save the ship.
2) God comes through this episode deserving of praise, but not us. We are shown to be petty, selfish, and foolish.
3) We have to finish our voyage with a lot of angry sailors who lost everything on account of us.

Sometimes living with the consequences of our actions is more than we want to endure. Yet the question of mercy persists.

- Do the heathen sailors deserve God's mercy? What grudge do we hold against them that we, who have the power to save them, should choose to let them die? Do we want to incur God's wrath for shedding innocent blood as a result of our sin?

- Seeing as how we have become no better than the heathen, do *we* deserve God's mercy? We are all in the same boat now. Disaster for them is disaster for us. Mercy for them is mercy for us.

Which do we choose—mercy or sacrifice, life or death?

"Choose life," God whispers in our ear. "I am a merciful God. If you repent, all will be forgiven and forgotten." In this moment, God brings us to the final objective of the lesson:

God's Objective #4: Teach us to desire mercy and show mercy to others, if only for our own sake.

Even so, we remain stubbornly rebellious and resist God's lesson.

The Decision

The sailors ask us what they should do with us. Do we deserve mercy from the heathen sailors? We have to find a solution. As we see it, our choices are:

1) Humble ourselves, pray, and maybe everyone lives (but then we have to finish the journey with those people and deal with the consequences.)
2) Keep quiet and everyone dies.
3) Sacrifice our own lives so that others might live. Let us die to save the rest.

We choose the third option. We are going to sacrifice ourselves so that they might live. This seems the perfect middle ground. We are showing a small amount of mercy to these sailors by taking ourselves out of their midst; but at the same time, we have not capitulated to God's authority. We would rather die than go to Nineveh. We would rather die than have to live with the consequences of our actions. In our pride and rebellion, we decide it is better to die than humble ourselves before God and repent.

Our choice to seek death is self-serving, but this is our choice. So we tell the sailors to throw us overboard and thus escape the storm.

They don't think this is a good solution. They resist sending us to our death and keep rowing for a while. They wrestle with their conscience and the fear of taking innocent blood because they really can't find fault with us except that we have this issue with our God. Our religious issue isn't something they take offense over nor does it concern them, except that they are caught up in this storm. So in their eyes, we haven't really done anything worthy of death. When they find they cannot prevail against the tumult of the storm, they finally accept that they have no choice. They throw us over.

When we first started down this path of disobedience, did we ever imagine our rebellion would lead to our death?

We disappear into the water, and become dead to the world. The sailors think they have sent us to a watery grave, and we become a closed chapter in their lives. We are the story they tell friends and strangers and the moral example they use to teach their children. This wretched experience in our lives is immortalized for generations. But who cares, because we are dead. Right?

The Bigger Picture

Jonah chooses death for what appeared to be very self-serving reasons, and he could have chosen to throw himself overboard rather than ask the sailors to do it. That is one way to look at this episode. But maybe the Lord is using Jonah's choices in this moment to orchestrate events in a way that another picture comes out of it.

Earlier we talked about the ways prophets presented their messages. They either tell you directly, or they live out a picture of the events to come, i.e. their actions describe the details of the event. You can never dismiss the possibility that even when the prophets of God are at their very worst—in their meanest, most disobedient, most despairing moments—they are still being used to paint a picture of something in the future. Their actions are designed to make you ask the questions "What are you doing?" and "Why are you doing it?"

If you only look at their actions on the surface, as we did when we were in the sailors' shoes, what these prophets are doing may not make sense and we may dismiss them as being selfish, sinful, or just plain nuts. When you are living in the moment, it is hard to see God's greater plan unfolding, even when you know what to look for.

A greater picture is playing out in these events and continues to unfold in the chapters to come. It is a testament to God's wisdom, power, and sovereignty that He uses this earthen vessel—this man driven by his own base inclinations of rebellion and bad choices—to paint a picture of surpassing glory for Himself. But it is going to take breaking that earthen vessel before the final picture is complete.

Application

This was God's first lesson in mercy—putting Jonah in a position where he had to be merciful to those he had the power to hurt. What were some of the obstacles that kept Jonah from being more merciful to those sailors?

Here are some of the effects rebellion and disobedience have on our lives:

- Rebellion takes us out of the presence of God.
- When we cut ourselves off from God, we lose the source of such benefits as provision, rest, peace, refuge, and strength.
- When we replace God with an alternative source or rival, we step into idolatry and begin a pursuit of futile and fleeting things.
- Rebellion turns our focus inward on ourselves. Life becomes all about us, and we lose perspective on life.
- Rebellion impacts other relationships in our lives.
    - We bring our storm into other people's lives.
    - We become blind to the effects our behavior has on others.
    - We become blind to the sacrifices they make on our account.

Has rebellion in your life ever affected your relationships? If so, how?

Here are some red flags that serve as warnings to us:
- When people start asking things like "When are you going to wake up?"
- When people's reactions to us tell us that something is not right.
- When we cut off communication with God and others.
- When we feel a desire to hide.
- When we engage in avoidance behaviors like running away, sleeping, or using some external aids to tune out of life (i.e., in extreme cases, resorting to the oblivion of drugs or alcohol).

Do you see any of these red flags in your life?

Describe in your own words how the Lord see us in all this.

God has a grand plan in the works, and it includes us. He values us enough to pursue us when we walk away. He is merciful to us even when we are not faithful to Him. He accepts us as works-in-progress but keeps working to get us back on track with His plan.

Since God's first lesson in mercy does not have the desired effect on Jonah, God teaches the next level of the lesson—and Jonah learns what it is like to be at the mercy of others.

Jonah 2: Jonah and God

Same Lesson, Different Circumstance

Instead of being in Jonah's shoes this time, we are going to be observers and critics. Let's recap the objectives of God's lesson in mercy in regards to the storm and the sailors, because we will be going through the same lesson again:

1) To give us a taste of what it is like to be out of God's presence, and to see how the pleasures of this world are fleeting.
2) To show us that our disobedience makes us little better than the heathen we despise.
3) To get our acknowledgement of who we are and Who God is.
4) To teach us to desire mercy and show mercy to others, if only for our own sakes.

If Jonah learned anything from Objective #1, it is that living a worldly lifestyle has its share of consequences, and those consequences have led to death. God gave him a rude awakening through the captain's words, and his pursuit of those tangible worldly treasures ended abruptly. As a result, he lost everything, even the intangible benefits he had from God like peace, rest, and well-being.

When we, as ambassadors for God, fail to understand the benefits of His presence in our lives, then we fail to communicate those benefits to the unbelieving world around us. As a result, the benefits are lost—not just for ourselves but for the world as well—and we doom others to living eternally outside the presence of God.

God gave his prophet another rude awakening with Objective #2, as Jonah found himself in the same boat, sharing the same fate as the heathen he despised. Rebellion brought him to an identity crisis as it does for us as well. If we are not ambassadors for God, who are we? The only thing that separates us from the world is our identity and relationship with God.

Objective #2 was quickly followed by Objective 3, where Jonah had to decide who he was and Who God was. God confronted him with the hypocrisy of calling himself a Hebrew while acting like a heathen.

Although God forced the verbal acknowledgement out of His ambassador, that didn't mean Jonah was going along with His plan. In Jonah's eyes, he was still master of his own fate, and he exercised that authority over his life in deciding to die. He thought it was his decision, when in reality, the Lord put him in the position of having to make that choice. He was not going to let Jonah stay in limbo on the ship. Jonah was going to either return to the land or go all the way into the sea.

In Scripture, the land is symbolic of Israel while the sea symbolizes the Gentile nations. It is curious that Jonah's choice to enter the sea can be taken symbolically as a decision to immerse himself in the Gentile nations, of Tarshish or Nineveh. From what we know of Jonah's fate, does he ever return to Israel?

For ourselves, keep in mind that when we choose to immerse ourselves in the world apart from God, it leads to death. Living in that sea depends on our own strength, which gives out eventually without provision and rest.

In this moment of decision, Jonah displays a grudging amount of mercy toward the sailors, which is God's final objective; but the lesson is not learned to the fullest extent God desires. The lesson does not achieve an inward change of Jonah's heart attitude or an outward show of obedience, nor does it re-establish a conviction that God is sovereign in his life.

Therefore, God is not done with this lesson.

He loves Jonah and pursues him with patience and persistence. He wants him to be His ambassador, so that people look at Jonah and see God in him. Jonah is part of God's unfolding plan, but he cannot be part of that plan until he has learned the value of mercy.

What is true of God's feelings toward Jonah is true of God's feelings toward us.

He doesn't want us to show mercy to people only because He is forcing us to do so. He wants us to *desire* mercy for others, even ISIS terrorists, in the same way God Himself desires to be merciful. He wants us to see people the way He sees them, even if they are Ninevites in our lives. He wants mercy to come from a heart attitude and not a sense of obligation.

It is the heart attitude God must ultimately address, because it is the heart attitude that leads to the act of disobedience. A wrong attitude leads to wrong action, which leads to challenging God's authority and sovereignty. God corrects these things in this order:

1) He re-establishes Who He is in Jonah's life. This becomes the first thing God must accomplish, for the sake of His sovereignty.

2) Then He tackles the next issue of turning Jonah from disobedience to obedience (at least in his actions). God must have Jonah's obedience, with or without the right heart attitude, for the sake of His plan. Jonah has a crucial role to play in the events that are swiftly unfolding. The decision for obedience is accomplished here in Jonah 2, and followed through in Jonah 3, as the prophet delivers God's message to the Ninevites.

3) Finally, God addresses the heart attitude in Jonah 4.

The lesson isn't really learned with the sailors, so God takes Jonah back through the same objectives again with greater intensity, as God goes head-to-head with Jonah in the isolation of the belly of a great fish. This time, instead of having a group of sailors at his mercy, the roles will be reversed and Jonah is at God's mercy.

Into the Fish

Because he does not appreciate the benefits he has as a child of God . . . Because he does not understand what it is like to live outside God's presence . . . Because he failed to be God's ambassador, to show mercy to others and spare them from an eternity outside of God's presence . . .

. . . God prepares a fish.

> *"Now the LORD had prepared a great fish to swallow Jonah. And Jonah was in the belly of the fish three days and three nights."—Jonah 1:17*

Return to Objective #1: What it is like to be out of God's presence.

Jonah sinks in the sea. He looks up and sees the light of day grow dimmer as the waters close over him and gives himself up to death.

How long can a person hold his breath? One minute? Maybe a couple minutes tops? (Being asthmatic, I cannot hold my breath for more than a minute!)

That fish was obviously waiting for Jonah.

Jonah sees a dark shape rushing at him through the water, and in a minute, it swallows him whole. The next thing he knows, he is awash in the dark, stinking, wet belly of the fish. He should be dead but is still alive. God purposely sent this rescue vessel to preserve his life, and Jonah is now going to experience, consciously, what it is really like to live out of the presence of God.

Remember, God is the source of light, rest, provision, peace, refuge (escape), strength, and life. Consider what it is like to be in the belly of a fish.

There is no light in the belly of a fish. It is just a limitless darkness, and without a visual reference to help Jonah get his bearing, the emptiness must seem vast. There is no sense of time, or passing of time, whether its day or night. But then God is the One Who gives light.

There is no rest or peace in the belly of the fish. There's nowhere to sit or lie down, unless Jonah wants to lie down in the muck. There is no relief from being constantly bumped around by the movement of the fish. But then God is the One Who gives rest and relief.

There is no provision for food or drink, short of what washes into the disposal of the fish's belly. So Jonah begins a time of enforced fasting. God lets Jonah's physical hunger drive his desire to return to God.

There is no escape or rescue from the belly of the fish. He cannot even kill himself to put an end to it. It is like a living death.

This is what eternity apart from God is like.

Death isn't the end of anything. It is just the beginning of a new reality. The fullest expression of dying and being separated from God is hell. Being in the fish is as close as a living person gets to that reality.

When Jonah refused to extend God's mercy and salvation to the sailors, he was dooming them to this kind of existence for eternity.

Would we really wish this on our worst enemy?

After three days and three nights, this experience in the fish does its work on Jonah. He has been living without light, rest, provision, escape, and peace, and his life is a living death. He now understands what it means to live apart from God.

After three days, God brings Jonah to an understanding of Who He is and who Jonah is. It is God's desire to re-establish the relationship between Himself and Jonah, and turn a disobedient man into an obedient one.

Jonah's Turning

All the time Jonah was on the boat, he never once spoke to God. Now he breaks his silence, and begins to communicate with God in earnest. His prayer is the beginning of his return to God.

> "Then Jonah prayed to the LORD his God from the fish's belly. And he said: 'I cried out to the LORD because of my affliction, and He answered me. Out of the belly of Sheol I cried, and You heard my voice.

For You cast me into the deep, into the heart of the seas, and the floods surrounded me; all Your billows and Your waves passed over me.

Then I said, 'I have been cast out of Your sight; Yet I will look again toward Your holy temple.'

The waters surrounded me, even to my soul; the deep closed around me; Weeds were wrapped around my head. I went down to the moorings of the mountains; the earth with its bars closed behind me forever; yet You have brought up my life from the pit, O LORD, my God.

When my soul fainted within me, I remembered the LORD; and my prayer went up to You, into Your holy temple.

Those who regard worthless idols forsake their own Mercy. But I will sacrifice to You with the voice of thanksgiving; I will pay what I have vowed. Salvation is of the LORD.'"—Jonah 2:1-9

The first thing we should note is that none of these words are original to Jonah. All these verses come from the Psalms and are strung together to make this prayer. It is interesting what psalms he chooses and how he sees himself in these psalms. In a moment of crisis, have you ever had Scripture verses come to mind? These are the ones that Jonah remembers. Sometimes it's just a snatch of a phrase from one psalm, but the rest of the psalm has little context with the moment. Other verses, though, are highly significant in their greater context.

I want to walk through these verses one at a time, and look at the psalms from which they are pulled to see what additional context these verses lend to the narrative.

Application:

Before we begin, I just want to say that, in a modern application, if you are in rebellion and out of step with God, it can be hard to start that conversation again. Praying through the Psalms is a good way to begin. The words of King David and the Psalmists speak from the heart about all different experiences and circumstances. They are Spirit-inspired words that please God and provide intercession for us. When we pray through the Psalms, even if we only pray snatches of verses, it helps correct our thinking and bows our hearts toward God. So if you have a hard time starting to pray, you might try reading through the Psalms. God eventually wants to hear from you in your own words, but the Psalms can be an icebreaker. Now let's work through Jonah's prayer.

Jonah's Prayer

Jonah 2:2a "I cried out to the LORD because of my affliction, and He answered me..."

Funny how once Jonah got what he wanted—to be out of God's presence—he found it to be an affliction to him. He really didn't know what he was asking for. The same could be said of us at times.

Jonah begins with this quote from Psalm 120.

Psalm 120:1 "A Song of Ascents. In my distress I cried to the LORD, and He heard me."

Jonah doesn't quite quote this verbatim, but it is very close. The rest of the psalm adds little context to what Jonah is going through, but what is interesting is where this verse fits in Jewish liturgy. When would a Jewish person recite this verse?

It is the first verse in a series of psalms called the Psalms of Ascent, and pilgrims coming to Jerusalem for the festivals would begin reciting these psalms as they climbed the hill toward Jerusalem, toward God in His Temple.

This verse is the one you begin with when you are at the bottom of the hill. The bottom of the hill is where Jonah sees himself.

Jonah 2:2b "Out of the belly of Sheol I cried, and You heard my voice."

Jonah is in the belly of the fish, which reminds him of this psalm about being in the belly of Sheol. There is a lot of imagery here. The word "belly" is the Hebrew word *beten*, meaning the deepest internal parts, a place of deep emotion, hollowness, emptiness, and hunger—quite fitting in Jonah's present circumstances.

Sheol is the Hebrew word for a place likened to hell. It also translates as the grave, the pit, or place of exile. It is a place of no return, where the wicked are sent for punishment. Proverbs 30:15b-16 associates Sheol with the grave, a barren womb, a land in drought, and a perpetual fire—all things which have continual demands that are never satisfied.

After three days in the belly of this fish, Jonah finally breaks his silence and speaks. He calls to God from a place of emptiness and hunger, and from a place of exile from which he believes there is no return. This is not just a place of physical darkness and emptiness, but also spiritual darkness and emptiness. The physical hunger in his own belly reflects a spiritual hunger to be back in the presence of the Lord. He cries out to God with all his voice from the *beten*, a place of deep emotion. Imagine how it must have echoed in that isolation. God has finally engaged Jonah's heart attitude.

Jonah is drawing from Psalm 18:5-6b for this, but I want to add the surrounding verses to give you the context that Jonah had in mind.

> *Psalm 18:4-6 "The pangs of death surrounded me, and the floods of ungodliness made me afraid. The sorrows of Sheol surrounded me; the snares of death confronted me. In my distress I called upon the LORD, and cried out to my God; He heard my voice from His temple, and my cry came before Him, even to His ears."*

There is a second psalm that also speaks of being in Sheol.

> *Psalm 16:10 "For You will not leave my soul in Sheol, nor will You allow Your Holy One to see corruption."*

We know that Jonah's three-day stint in this fish becomes a sign for a future generation. When Jesus speaks to the Pharisees of His death and resurrection, He points them to this episode in Jonah where Jonah quotes the psalm that speaks of not being left in *Sheol* to see corruption. Jonah's words invoke this psalm that has a deeper layer of prophetic meaning to it. In the Jewish mind, it rings a bell.

Jonah 2:3a "For You cast me into the deep, into the heart of the seas, and the floods surrounded me;"

This verse comes from Psalm 69:2, but consider the context.

> *Psalm 69:1-3 ". . . Save me, O God! For the waters have come up to my neck. I sink in deep mire, where there is no standing; I have come into deep waters, where the floods overflow me. I am weary with my crying; my throat is dry; My eyes fail while I wait for my God."*

This particular psalm continues on.

> *Psalm 69:5-9 "O God, You know my foolishness; and my sins are not hidden from You. Let not those who wait for You, O Lord GOD of hosts, be ashamed because of me; let not those who seek You be confounded because of me, O God of Israel. Because for Your sake I have borne reproach; Shame has covered my face. I have become a stranger to my brothers, and an alien to my mother's children; because zeal for Your house has eaten me up, and the reproaches of those who reproach You have fallen on me."*

In the greater context of this psalm, we see the beginnings of a confession that could easily apply to Jonah. "You know my foolishness . . . my sins are not hidden . . . Shame has covered my face." Jonah has become estranged to his own people. Why? *"Because zeal for Your house has eaten me up."*

Let's forget for a moment that these words were applied to Jesus, and just think about how Jonah has been zealous for God. I think Jonah remembers this psalm because he sees himself as being zealous for the Lord in his heart.

Is it good to be zealous for God in hating the things God hates?

Can our hatred of certain sins keep us from engaging people the way the Lord wants us to engage them?

Jonah thinks he is doing a good thing by hating the pagan, wicked Ninevites, but does his zeal lead him to the correct behavior?

There is a zeal derived from hatred that causes us to punish people and leave them unreconciled in their sin, and there is a zeal derived from love that delivers punishment in order to bring healing and a right relationship with God.

Zeal born of hatred is what Jonah illustrates. Jonah's zeal leads him to shun sinful people and have nothing to do with them. He keeps his distance and lets them suffer the consequences of sin.

Zeal born of love is what Jesus illustrated. This same Psalm is quoted in John 2:17, in the account of Jesus cleansing the Temple by driving out the money changers. Jesus's zeal led him to confront the sinful behavior, deliver punishment that was necessary *to drive them to repentance*, and restore them to right relationship with God. That is the correct role of a *tsiyr*, an ambassador who brings pain for a moment so that healing may happen.

Zeal for the Lord that leads to confrontation with people often ends with the reproach being heaped on the head of the messenger. In this world, we will suffer reproach from men for the stance we take on sin. But we should never suffer reproach from the Lord for not engaging a sinful world.

Jonah 2:3b "...all Your billows and Your waves passed over me."

This is a fairly straightforward quote of Psalm 42:7.

> *Psalm 42:7b "Deep calls unto deep at the noise of Your waterfalls; All Your waves and billows have gone over me."*

In its greater context, this psalm speaks of being hungry and thirsty for the

Lord. *"As the deer pants for the water, so pants my soul for You, O God ... My tears have been my food day and night..."* (Psalm 42:1, 3) It speaks repeatedly of a soul cast down in despair, having been forgotten by God, and yet there is hope. At this point, there is a turning from despair to hope.

> **Jonah 2:4** *"Then I said, 'I have been cast out of Your sight; Yet I will look again toward Your holy temple.'"*

When Jonah says he will look "toward Your holy temple," he may be imagining the Temple in Jerusalem; but often in the Scripture, God's holy Temple is referring to God's *heavenly* Temple. As Jonah sinks into the sea, we imagine him looking back up to the surface—to the light above shining through the watery depths—and thinking of God in His heavenly Temple. That is the last image he sees before the fish swallows him up. The distance between God and Jonah is very great, and God seems very remote.

Jonah quotes from Psalm 31. In its greater context, it says:

> *Psalm 31:9-12, 22 "Have mercy on me, O LORD, for I am in trouble; my eye wastes away with grief, my soul and my body! For my life is spent with grief, and my years with sighing; my strength fails because of my iniquity, and my bones waste away. I am a reproach among all my enemies, but especially among my neighbors, and am repulsive to my acquaintances; those who see me outside flee from me. I am forgotten like a dead man, out of mind; I am like a broken vessel. . . . For I said in my haste, 'I am cut off from before Your eyes'; Nevertheless You heard the voice of my supplications when I cried out to You."*

If we apply the greater context of this passage to Jonah's condition, we see the confession of brokenness. He is a broken vessel. What he has done has broken not only his relationship with God, but with the human relationships in his life. He is repulsive even to acquaintances—those sailors who threw him overboard and have forgotten him as a dead man. It's broken his relationship with his own people as well. He has had to leave his land. He has reached a point of acknowledging the brokenness in his life.

> **Jonah 2:5-6a** *"The waters surrounded me, even to my soul; the deep closed around me; weeds were wrapped around my head. I went down to the moorings of the mountains; the earth with its bars closed behind me forever; Yet You have brought up my life from the pit, O LORD, my God."*

These verses describe how far he falls in his rebellion. He goes down to the depths of the earth. Jonah quotes diverse parts of Psalm 88, which is a psalm given over to the contemplation of weakness, affliction of soul, and humbling. How very appropriate for Jonah to be thinking about this as he comes to this low point.

In Psalm 88:10, there is an appeal to God in this moment of brokenness, with overtones of resurrection and restoration: *"Will You work wonders for the dead? Shall the dead arise and praise You?"* This follows into the second half of Jonah 2:6b, that speaks of a life brought up from the pit, where Jonah quotes from Psalm 30.

> *Psalm 30:2-3 "O LORD my God, I cried out to You, and You healed me. O LORD, You brought my soul up from the grave; You have kept me alive, that I should not go down to the pit."*

Psalm 88 and 30 have the common theme of resurrection and restoration. We should note that the Hebrew word for "pit" in Psalm 30:3 is not *Sheol* as we studied earlier. "Pit" here means tomb, sepulcher, or prison (dry pits or dry cisterns were used as prisons). It is also the word for "corruption" used in Psalm 16:10 *"For You will not leave my soul in Sheol, nor will You allow Your Holy One to see corruption."* Again, these psalms are heavy with Messianic themes.

> **Jonah 2:7 "When my soul fainted within me, I remembered the LORD; and my prayer went up to You, into Your holy temple."**

Jonah brings us back to Psalm 18:6 again.

Even the depths of the earth are not too far away for God in heaven to see Jonah and hear his cry. And so he looks to God for his deliverance.

Throughout Jonah's prayer, there is a contrast between Jonah who is very low, and God Who is very high up in heaven. Jonah calls out across the vast expanse separating the depths and heights. No matter how high in the heavens God is, Jonah believes God still hears his prayer.

There is a psalm that goes with this thought.

> *Psalm 103:11-12 "For as the heavens are high above the earth, [So] great is His mercy toward those who fear Him; as far as the east is from the west, [So] far has He removed our transgressions from us."*

Jonah doesn't quote this, but it is worth noting because it highlights the contrast in distance between God and the condition of man.

> *Jonah 2:8 "Those who regard worthless idols forsake their own mercy."*

> *Psalm 31:6 "I have hated those who regard useless idols; but I trust in the LORD."*

"Idols" are a translation of the Hebrew word, *hebel*, meaning vapor, breath, or vanity—something fleeting and without substance. So, the verse could be translated "Those who regard worthless vapors forsake their own mercy." The pursuit of *hebel* is like grasping at the merciless wind.

Jonah looks back at the "vapors" of his life—the fruitless pursuit of things that disappeared like a cloud over the course of a single day. He remembers watching the heathen sailors throw their cargo overboard, trying to obtain mercy from gods that don't exist. He remembers the futility of what they were doing, and comes to the conviction that, in serving worthless idols, they forsook the one true God Who would show them mercy. God was their Mercy.

Jonah starts down that path to becoming like those sailors in his worldly pursuits by seeking other means of attaining those things apart from God. But now, all of these things have come to nothing. They benefit Jonah nothing, just as they benefit the sailors nothing. The things in which he once trusted forsake him. They are just vanities, gone like a vapor. All this time, he has been grasping at the wind.

The sacrifice of these things, even of Jonah's life, is not the sacrifice God desires. There is nothing in this fish to offer as a sacrifice, save what comes from Jonah's own lips. So now Jonah offers a different kind of sacrifice.

> *Jonah 2:9 "But I will sacrifice to You with the voice of thanksgiving; I will pay what I have vowed. Salvation is of the LORD."*

Sacrifices of praise, paying vows, and receiving salvation from God are all reflected in Psalm 50.

> *Psalm 50:12-14, 22-23 "If I [God] were hungry, I would not tell you; for the world is Mine, and all its fullness. Will I eat the flesh of bulls, or drink the blood of goats? Offer to God thanksgiving, and pay your vows to the Most High. . . . Now consider this, you who forget God, or I will tear you in pieces, and there will be none to deliver. He who offers a sacrifice of thanksgiving honors Me; and to him who orders his way aright I shall show the salvation of God."*

> *Psalm 3:8 "Salvation belongs to the LORD. Your blessing is upon Your people. Selah"*

Out of all the sacrifices that Jonah could give, a sacrifice of thanksgiving is a very acceptable gift in the eyes of the Lord. Every physical thing on this earth is God's to begin with. When we sacrifice physical things, we are only giving back to God something He has given to us. But there is one thing in life that God does not own and cannot take by His own power or will unless we give it to Him, and that is our words of praise and thanksgiving. These come uniquely from each of us, and are only born out of our understanding of Who God is. Out of all the sacrifices we can make, the ones God covets most of all are our praise and thanksgiving.

Jonah comes to an understanding of Who God is in his life. He admits his own weakness and humbles himself in acknowledgment. That is a good first step toward repentance.

Paying ones vows is akin to *"him who orders his way aright."* They are the things that you do to honor God. *"He who orders his way aright"* has different translations in different Bible versions, but it generally means to get one's life back on the right path or the right journey. Jonah has been on a journey in the wrong direction. All this time, he has been on a downward path into disobedience, and now he is turning spiritually and physically on a path in the opposite direction. That, by Hebrew definition, is repentance—the act of turning around. To the man who turns, God shows salvation. For Jonah, part of that turning includes paying what he has vowed. He is a prophet of God, which means he has an agreement with God to act as His ambassador. If God graciously offers him salvation, he is heading for Nineveh. This is the psalm Jonah thinks about, and he comes to a very personal understanding of it.

This acknowledgement of Who God is and who Jonah is accomplished the first point God addresses in Jonah's life. The second point is to deal with the action—to turn disobedience to obedience so that Jonah fulfills the plan God destined for him. This is what we see happening when Jonah agrees to pay what he has vowed. The last point God deals with is the heart attitude. We'll come to that in the next chapters.

When we reach this point in our lives, we may not think God is there, but God is still present, and He is going through this with us. He is just being very quiet. He does this with Jonah, and He does this with us. When our rebellion throws us into troubled waters, God may intervene enough to keep us from self-destruction; but then He takes Himself out of view for a while so that we can experience the full impact of our choices. He lets us experience fear, loneliness, and even severe discomfort. We need the fish experience to understand the reality of it, if we are to learn a lasting lesson. But He hasn't abandoned us. He is waiting silently in the dark, ready to offer mercy the moment we submit and turn back to Him.

> *"So the LORD spoke to the fish, and it vomited Jonah onto dry land."*
> *—Jonah 2:10*

God's mercy and forgiveness are complete and instantaneous. There are no lingering conditions or consequences. He doesn't keep Jonah in the fish a second longer as punishment. He restores him.

Application and Reflection

Have you ever used the Psalms in your own private life for prayer or worship? If so, is there a Psalm that has special meaning to you?

Have you ever identified with Jonah's zeal in hating the things that God hates? If so, how did your zeal translate into words or actions?

Did your zeal bring glory to God or convey His mercy?

Describe an experience equivalent to being in the belly of the fish.

What has to happen inside a person for them to give thanks to God from that place in their life?

A Critique of Jonah's Prayer

Before we move on, I want to take one more look at Jonah's prayer. Jonah said some right things in this prayer, but there are a few things he didn't say.

Those of us who have raised children know that when a child under discipline says, "I am sorry," sometimes parents need to press them a little further by asking "What are you sorry for?" You ask yourself, "Does the child really understand what they did wrong or what the problem was? Do they understand the consequences of it? Do they understand the lesson?"

From Jonah's prayer, what does Jonah consider his sin was?

Is there a sense of conscience or remorse for his behavior toward the sailors and the negative consequences it had for them? Does he mention the Ninevites at all?

Are there other things of which Jonah might have repented?

Does Jonah's prayer reflect a self-focused or others-focused attitude?

How do your prayers compare with Jonah's?

    a. Do you often confess a sin in particular or just sin in general?

    b. Do you think of who else might have been hurt by your attitudes or actions?

    c. Do you acknowledge the harm you have caused others?

Has Jonah learned the lessons of mercy God set out to teach him?

Jonah acknowledges God's sovereignty and promises to be obedient, but his heart attitude still hasn't changed. Jonah feels an obligation to God, but not a desire to be like Him in character. The heart attitude comes to the forefront in the chapters to come.

Critics of the Fish

Critics say that the story of Jonah is made up because there couldn't possibly be a fish big enough to swallow a man and have him survive for three days. There is no physical proof that this fish is real—but then there is no proof that this fish isn't real either. Even if a sailor or fisherman sees a fish this size, would anyone believe him if he says, "I saw a fish THIS BIG!" That is just the kind of fish story every fisherman tells, and it would be dismissed as an exaggeration.

We might ask critics, why throw one allegorical element into a story that is otherwise historically real?

We know Jonah is real. We read in 2 Kings 14:25 that he gives a prophecy to King Jeroboam of Israel and it comes true. So Jonah is tied to a very real king at a very real time in history. This is not a parable that starts out "Once upon a time . . ." There is even a tomb for Jonah in Mosul, Iraq, the site of ancient Nineveh. News reports have shown that ISIS terrorists encamped at Mosul damaged and defaced it. If Jonah has a tomb, then at some point he must have died physically. If he died, then he must have lived. No one makes tombs for imaginary characters in a story.

Jesus claims that Jonah is real, and the three days and nights Jonah spends in the belly of the fish were meant to be a sign of Jesus' death and resurrection after three days; and Jesus' resurrection did happen, as prophesied.

The sailors of the ships of Tarshish are real. The Ninevites are real. Archeological evidence, which I talk about in the next chapter, shows the events happening in Nineveh around the time of Jonah are real and support Jonah's story.

So if all the rest of the story is real, why not the fish? Why throw in one allegorical element into a story that is otherwise historically real?

Rebellion causes us to question Who God is and who we are. Is God really the Creator? Can God really make a giant fish just for the purpose of a lesson on mercy? Does He have power over our lives? Does He have the right to demand we deliver our vows and be His ambassadors as we agree to do as part of our relationship with Him?

Yes, He can; and yes, He does.

Jonah 3: Jonah and the Ninevites

FROM THE NINEVITES' PERSPECTIVE

"Now the word of the LORD came to Jonah the second time, saying, 'Arise, go to Nineveh, that great city, and preach to it the message that I tell you.' So Jonah arose and went to Nineveh, according to the word of the LORD. Now Nineveh was an exceedingly great city, a three-day journey in extent."
—*Jonah 3:1-3*

God is so merciful in His forgetfulness.

Chapter 3 opens exactly as Chapter 1 did—God just picks up again in Jonah's life almost as if the disobedience, storm, and fish never happened. Jonah has been through lessons in mercy, suffered God's discipline, and repented. Now God says, "Let's start again and move on." The mission hasn't changed, and deep down Jonah's attitude hasn't changed either, but this time, Jonah goes along with the plan and is determined to get the job done. So he begins walking to Nineveh.

Even if the fish dropped Jonah off closer to Nineveh, it is still going to take the prophet about a month to walk there. A month's walk will give Jonah ample time to reflect on those lessons, and perhaps this question will come to mind: Why is God so concerned with Nineveh and the Assyrian people?

Jonah won't get an answer to that question, but we know from history that God used the Assyrians to deal with the disobedient northern kingdom of Israel, which had become exceedingly wicked, arrogant, and idolatrous. When the northern kingdom of Israel split apart from the southern kingdom of Judah, it replaced all the God-ordained worship places, practices, and even the priesthood with its own version of those things. They even replaced God Himself with idols; therefore, to re-establish His sovereignty, God sent them out of the land.

Jonah is a prophet from that northern kingdom. At the time God sends him to Nineveh, the kingdom of Israel is only one generation away from captivity. That means the children of this generation of Ninevites are the ones to take Israel down.

If God just turned Assyria loose on Israel as they are, Assyria would completely destroy Israel. He wants Israel chastised to the point of repentance, but not destroyed. God's purpose in sending Jonah to Nineveh is to put the fear of Himself in the Assyrians—to bring them to an understanding of Who He is, who His people are, and the need to restrain themselves in the role God gives them. If the Assyrians of Nineveh fear God, they might act more circumspectly with His people; but if the Assyrians don't restrain themselves, then He holds them accountable for it. God is establishing a relationship with these heathen people for the sake of His disobedient children, while extending mercy to the Assyrians themselves through Jonah.

Let's look at what we know about Nineveh and its people in Jonah's day.

Nineveh

The earliest biblical reference to Nineveh is in Genesis 10:8-12. Its builder, Nimrod, was a mighty builder and hunter, and hunting was in the blood of the Assyrian people. They are renowned as a race of fierce, brutal, aggressive hunters and warriors who glorify war and violence. From the remnants of artwork that archeologists have unearthed, the Assyrians' two favorite pastimes appear to be making war and hunting lions. This part of their identity and character as a people makes them the perfect weapon, with tempering, in the Lord's hand.

Moving forward from Genesis, Nineveh is not mentioned again in Scripture until the book of Jonah on the eve of Israel's captivity, nor is it mentioned afterward until the book of Nahum, written about 100 years after Jonah at the end of Assyria's history as a world empire. Nahum prophesies against Nineveh, which is followed by Assyria's fall to Babylonia in 612 B.C. There is a bit of divine nose-tweaking in Assyria's demise, in that the lion killers of Assyria are swallowed by the great lion of Babylon, as Daniel 7:4 describes.

Nineveh appears for a very short, specific time in Bible history with a very specific purpose.

By the time of Jonah, Nineveh is one of the Assyrian Empire's three preeminent cities. Built on the eastern banks of the Tigris River, Nineveh is called the "great city" four times (Jonah 1:2, 3:2, 3:3, 4:11). It is big, imposing, fortified with great thick walls carved with lions and fearsome creatures, and heavily populated, having at minimum 120,000 persons as mentioned in Jonah 4. Great cities in the Bible are often the royal cities, which is what Nineveh becomes as the Lord builds it up. The Lord Himself calls it a great city. It is great in size and imposing in its physical presence and political power as a seat of the authority in Assyria.

Jonah 3:3 says it was a "three-day journey in extent." There is some debate over what this means. This could refer to a three-day journey to walk around the perimeter of the city, making it approximately 60 to 80 miles around, or it could take three days to walk to the center of the city, making it exceedingly large.

The third possibility is that it takes three days to walk *through* the city, with the three-day journey divided into three stages: one day for arrival, one day for delivering the message, and one day for leaving. I favor this idea of passing through the city because that is what Jonah does in the narrative. He enters the city from the west on the first day, spends some time there, and then exits the city, still heading east. This also echoes the structure of the previous three days in the fish—a day of arrival, a day of reflection, and a day of leaving. It also echoes what the fish experience foreshadows—Jesus' three days in the grave: the day of His death, the day He spends in the grave and the day He comes out of the grave at His resurrection. So it seems consistent to interpret a three-day extent as passing through the city.

There is no definitive understanding of how large a city that three-day journey represents, but it is substantial.

The Historical Timeline

I previously mentioned what Jonah knew about Nineveh and how it tinted the way he saw the Ninevites. Sometimes we are swayed by what we think we know about people, but sometimes that is second-hand information or yesterday's news. We have a past with them, but we don't always know what is happening in current events, or how the Lord is working in their lives.

Such is the case with Jonah and the Ninevites.

Before we continue with the present narrative, let's step out of Jonah's shoes and look at the greater historical timeline of events in Nineveh leading up to the time of Jonah. To do that, we must begin by mentioning the reigning kings during this time period.

Jonah is tied to the reign of Jeroboam II, King of Israel (793–752 B.C.)[1] which overlaps with the reign of King Uzziah of Judah (791-739 B.C.),[2] and Ashur-dan III of Assyria (772–755 B.C.). Ashur-dan III is most likely the Assyrian king during Jonah's sojourn, but there is scholarly debate over why the narrative of Jonah describes the actions of a King of Nineveh, instead of the

---

1   This date is based on Thiele's chronology.

2   This dated is based on Thiele's chronology, supported by Britannica, where Uzziah is coregent with his father in the early part of his regnal years and coregent with his son Jotham in his late years after he is struck with leprosy. Thus he reigned 52 years, as per 2 Chronicles 26:3. Albright and Assyrian records have him reigning for 41 years from 783-742 B.C.

King of Assyria. Is this Ashur-dan III, and if so, why is he given a title as king over just a localized area? If we look at archaeological evidence of historical events in the reign of Ashur-dan III, it may shed light on this issue.

The Events in the Reign of Ashur-Dan III[3]

When archeologist unearthed Nineveh, they found a tremendous number of administrative records on everything from royal decrees to natural disasters. The Assyrians kept really good records of everything. Even so, there was a gap in the historical record that some scholars call the "40 lean years" in Assyrian history.[4] Many royal inscriptions and decrees were found before and after this time, but in between there is a significant gap in Assyrian historical records, coinciding with the reign of Ashur-dan III, a weak king who inherited the kingdom at the lowest point in its history. These were Assyria's Dark Ages. Here are some of the recorded events of Ashur-dan III's reign.

> **Civil Revolt:** The absence of royal decrees or governmental documents points to the widespread civil unrest and uprisings that plagued the Assyrian Empire from 783 to 754 B.C., beginning before and continuing throughout Ashur-dan III's reign. Wealthy nobles and provincial governors assumed power as kings over their own provinces and issued decrees as if they were royalty. They waged territorial campaigns and made monuments to their own exploits without any reference to or acknowledgement of the King of Assyria himself. Some of these territorial campaigns began to erode Israel's northern border, and we see in 2 Kings 14:25 where Jonah prophesies that Jeroboam II would re-establish that border. So, at this time, Assyria was under continually shifting leadership at a provincial level. This lends some support as to why the King of Nineveh, a provincial usurper, might be on the scene here in Jonah 3 instead of the King of Assyria.
>
> **Plagues & famines:** A seven-year period of Ashur-dan III's reign was marked by famine and plague (765–759 B.C.), which would have decimated the population and put the king's military out of commission.
>
> **Earthquake:** Archeological records revealed a significant earthquake happened during the reign of Ashur-dan III that was noted on one of the

---

3 Wiseman, Donald J., *Jonah's Nineveh*, The Tyndale Biblical Archaeology Lecture, 1977, *Tynedale Bulletin* 30 (1979) p.29-52.

4 Ferguson, Paul. "Who Was the 'King of Nineveh' in Jonah 3:6?". *Tyndale Bulletin* 47.2 (November 1996) p.311

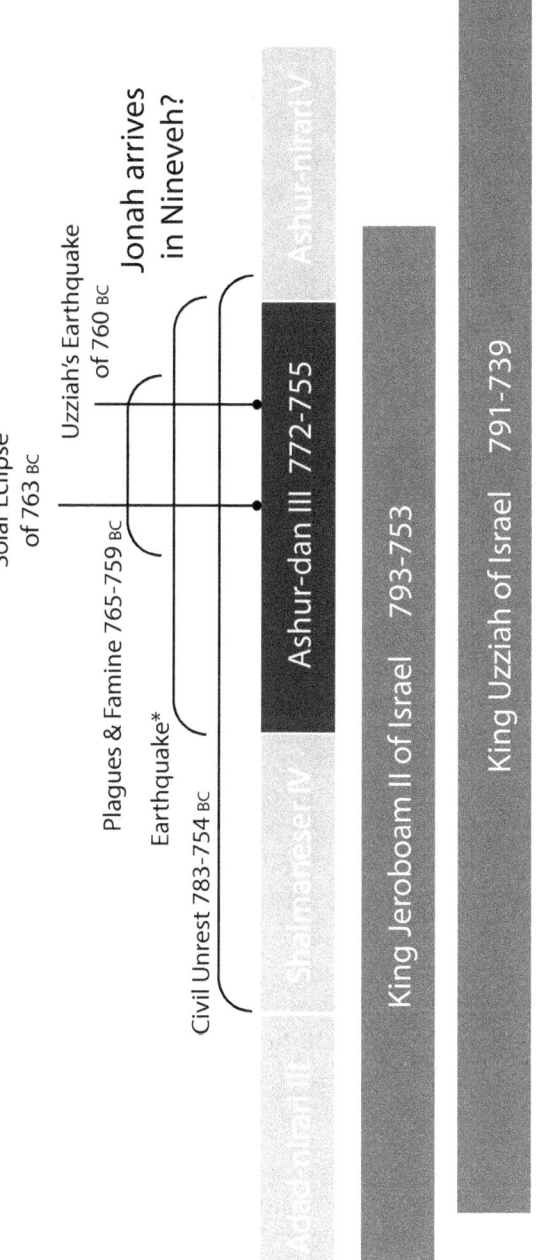

Jonah 3: Jonah and the Ninevites | 71

Assyrian tablets. Unfortunately, the year was missing on the inscription, but it did mention the month—Sivan. In pagan cultures, earthquakes in general were interpreted as signs of divine wrath.

Solar eclipse of 763 B.C.: Solar eclipses were especially recorded because they were considered ill omens for king and country—portending either the death of a king or the overthrow of a dynasty or city. These records included interpretations of these events, describing the effects the divine wrath would have on the city, the people, even the animals during this time, and recording what actions were prescribed to respond to these events.

Plagues, famines, earthquakes, and a major solar eclipse were all indicators that an explosion of divine wrath was on the horizon for Ashur-dan III's kingdom. If there was ever a time for a prophet of God to walk out of the wilderness into that great city with a message that imminent overthrow was about to take place—and for him to be taken seriously—it would have been somewhere during this time. We may not be able to place Jonah definitively on the timeline, but looking at the confluence of events and the people's reaction to Jonah, it would seem an educated guess to place him during the reign of this king. I would even speculate he showed up around the time of the great solar eclipse of 763 B.C. for the following reason.

The Sar Puhi Ritual[5]

Whenever a solar eclipse happened in ancient times and pagan nations, the religious leaders, soothsayers, and astrologers would record the event, interpret it, and suggest a way of avoiding or subverting the divine wrath it portended. During the full solar eclipse of 763 B.C., historical records show a particular ritual called the *sar puhi* ("substitute king") was prescribed and enacted. This ritual began with a time of solemn fasting for people and animals alike, during which time the reigning king (like Ashur-dan) would hand over the throne to a substitute king who would take upon himself the consequences of the divine wrath about to fall. The real king would withdraw from public life and remain in his palace until the danger was over. A set number of days would be determined until the demise of the substitute king.

This ritual is found in Assyrian, Babylonian, Akkadian, and Hittite records and was a common practice in those cultures. According to the Ninevite letter

---

5   Wiseman, Donald J., *Jonah's Nineveh*, The Tyndale Biblical Archaeology Lecture, 1977, *Tyndale Bulletin* 30 (1979) p.47.

archives, this ritual was prescribed for the solar eclipse of 763 B.C. and a description of it was given.

In the book of Jonah, there is much scholarly debate over why the king is called the King of Nineveh and not the King of Assyria.[6] There was an Assyrian king on the throne at the time, so why is he given a localized dominion over just Nineveh? Some attribute this to the civil unrest and shifting provincial powers at the time, but others point out the similarities between the *sar puhi* ritual and what is being described in Jonah 3. Consider the parallels.

In Jonah 3:4, Jonah arrives in Nineveh declaring that in forty days, the city would be overthrown. So we have a number of days determined for the demise of the king, as with the *sar puhi* ritual.

In Jonah 3:5-6, the people immediately begin fasting and mourning, believing they are being given a divine warning. Jonah's message is then taken to the King of Nineveh. If the *sar puhi* ritual is in effect, it would explain why a lesser, localized king is on the throne, and not the King of Assyria. It says the king *"arose from his throne and laid aside his robe, covered himself in sackcloth and sat down in the ashes."* The king himself believes the report that his own life is doomed.

In Jonah 3:7-9 the King of Nineveh issues a decree. It is issued by both "the king and his nobles" which again indicates either a noble with his advisors have taken over the rule, or that the substitute king is acting under the direction of the real king's chief advisors in dealing with the crisis.

The decree prescribes a severe fast, not just for the people but for the animals as well, in keeping with the *sar puhi* ritual. Everyone is to be clothed in sackcloth, even the animals. Everyone is commanded to repent and turn from their violence and wicked ways in the hope that the divine wrath might relent.

Thus, there is strong evidence from the reactions of both the people and the king that a *sar puhi* ritual is in effect.

The confluence of natural disasters and Jonah's prophecy works the necessary change in the Assyrian people's heart, and they repent. It says they "believed God," which in our Bibles carries the capital "G," meaning Jehovah God; but the Hebrew word behind it is simply Elohim, which could indicate God, or gods in general, or even rulers. It is a word with a wide

---

6   Ferguson, Paul. "Who Was the 'King of Nineveh' in Jonah 3:6?". *Tyndale Bulletin* 47.2 (November 1996) p. 301-314.

range of connotations. I think perhaps Jonah's identity as a Hebrew is the clue that this is Jehovah Elohim Who is angry.

> *"Then God saw their works, that they turned from their evil way; and God relented from the disaster that He had said He would bring upon them, and He did not do it."— Jonah 3:10*

God is consistent when it comes to showing mercy, whether to the children of Israel, a bunch of heathen sailors, or even Ninevites.

Jonah's Prophecy

So here is an interesting question to ask in a Bible study class. If God relented in bringing disaster on Nineveh, does that mean Jonah's prophecy that Nineveh would be overthrown in 40 days went unfulfilled? The specific 40-day limit sets the deadline for when the prophecy had to be fulfilled and doesn't really allow for a later fulfillment or for judgment to be deferred on another generation. Is Jonah's prophecy fulfilled within the specified 40 days, so as not to make Jonah (or God) a liar?

The answer to that lies in a study of the Hebrew word translated as "overthrown." It is the word, *haphak*.

Haphak has some variations in its meaning. It can mean a people or nation being overthrown and brought to an end, as we see in these verses:

> *Genesis 19:21, 25, 29 "And he said to him, 'See, I have favored you concerning this thing also, in that I will not overthrow [haphak] this city for which you have spoken.' . . . So He overthrew [haphak] those cities, all the plain, all the inhabitants of the cities, and what grew on the ground. . . . And it came to pass, when God destroyed the cities of the plain, that God remembered Abraham, and sent Lot out of the midst of the overthrow, when He overthrew [haphak] the cities in which Lot had dwelt."*

> *Haggai 2:22 "I [the LORD] will overthrow [haphak] the throne of kingdoms; I will destroy the strength of the Gentile kingdoms. I will overthrow [haphak] the chariots and those who ride in them; the horses and their riders shall come down, everyone by the sword of his brother."*

Haphak has other meanings, though. It can also mean to turn and go in another direction, as in these verses:

> *Exodus 10:19 "And the LORD turned [haphak] a very strong west wind, which took the locusts away and blew them into the Red Sea. There remained not one locust in all the territory of Egypt."*

Judges 20:41 "And when the men of Israel turned back [haphak], the men of Benjamin panicked, for they saw that disaster had come upon them."

1 Samuel 25:12 "So David's young men turned [haphak] on their heels and went back; and they came and told him all these words."

It can also mean to have a change of character or condition:

Exodus 7:15, 17 "Go to Pharaoh in the morning, when he goes out to the water, and you shall stand by the river's bank to meet him; and the rod which was turned [haphak] to a serpent you shall take in your hand. . . . 'Thus says the LORD: "By this you shall know that I am the LORD. Behold, I will strike the waters which are in the river with the rod that is in my hand, and they shall be turned [haphak] to blood."'"

Psalms 30:11 "You have turned [haphak] for me my mourning into dancing; you have put off my sackcloth and clothed me with gladness,"

Psalms 32:4 "For day and night Your hand was heavy upon me; My vitality was turned [haphak] into the drought of summer."

Psalms 66:6 "He turned [haphak] the sea into dry land; they went through the river on foot. There we will rejoice in Him."

Most significantly, it can mean to have a change of heart, which I think is what applies to Nineveh in this moment. Look at some of the instances where *haphak* is used this sense:

Exodus 14:5 "Now it was told the king of Egypt that the people had fled, and the heart of Pharaoh and his servants was turned [haphak] against the people; and they said, 'Why have we done this, that we have let Israel go from serving us?'"

1 Samuel 10:6, 9 "Then the Spirit of the LORD will come upon you, and you will prophesy with them and be turned [haphak] into another man . . . So it was, when he had turned his back to go from Samuel, that God gave [haphak] him another heart; and all those signs came to pass that day."

Lamentations 1:20 "See, O LORD, that I am in distress; my soul is troubled; my heart is overturned [haphak] within me, for I have been very rebellious. Outside the sword bereaves, at home it is like death."

Job 19:19 "All my close friends abhor me, and those whom I love have turned [haphak] against me."

> *Psalms 105:25 "He turned [haphak] their heart to hate His people, to deal craftily with His servants."*

Now imagine for a moment that you are Jonah, and the Lord puts these words in your mouth to say to the Ninevites: *"Yet forty days, and Nineveh shall be* haphak-*ed!"* Privately, you might wonder just what the Lord means by that. Jonah, undoubtedly, desires something along the lines of Sodom and Gomorrah's overthrow; then again, he knows God could effect a change of condition or heart. As it turns out, the *haphak*-ing was an overthrow of heart. Thus the Lord fulfills the prophecy in a way that allows Him to extend mercy to the Ninevites without contradicting His word or His sovereignty.

Sadly, this change of heart does not last into future generations. We know from Nahum's prophecy that judgment will eventually fall on Nineveh, and they will be overthrown by Babylonia. But in this generation, the Lord accepts their act of repentance and defers judgment, according to His policy of mercy.

Application

From your own experience, what has to happen to effect not just a change of behavior but a change of heart in a person?

Have you ever had a haphak-*ing moment in your life?*

Jonah 4: Jonah and God, Again

Heart Attitude

God has been dealing with Jonah on three issues:

- The challenge to Who He is as God and who Jonah is as His servant. He dealt with that.
- The issue of disobedience in Jonah. He dealt with that.
- The heart attitude. This has not yet been dealt with. Jonah does what God wants him to do out of obligation, but not out of conviction.

Dealing with the heart attitude can be a difficult thing. Most of us are pretty good at hiding how we feel about people, especially when it involves a past hurt, grudge, or other resentment. We tend to bury these things deep inside us, and then do our best to just avoid the offenders. As long as we keep our distance from them or keep from engaging them directly, that heart attitude can remain dormant for a long, long time. When we bury resentments, grudges, and anger inside ourselves, they begin to eat away at us and make us miserable. For the sake of our spiritual health, God forces these issues out into the light. He does this to help us be holy from the inside out, to refine us and get that dross out of us.

When God sets out to deal with our heart attitude, first He brings that buried attitude to the surface. That means sending us among the very people we fear, hate, resent, or disdain, and letting them be the catalyst for that purpose. The minute we are forced to engage these people in our lives—talk to them, work with them, or share a space with them—all of a sudden those feelings rise to the surface and come out, sometimes in extreme emotion.

When God brings people into our lives, or sends us to them, we often think we are there to deal with their problems, when actually God is using them to bring our problems to light.

Such is the case with Jonah.

Anger

> *"But it displeased Jonah exceedingly, and he became angry."* —Jonah 4:1

The NKJV translation is a little tame. The Hebrew word for "displease" actually means to be trembling with anger—as if Jonah can hardly contain himself and is looking for something to smite. The Hebrew word for "angry" means to be incensed, to burn with rage. This isn't just dismay or frustration or being generally upset; this is a full blown, violent rage.

Let's look at how Jonah's anger has been building up:

- He was angry with the Ninevites before he was sent on the mission.
- He was really unhappy with the mission from the beginning.
- He went through a divinely-inspired storm and then spent three miserable days in a fish. God finally brought him to the point of grudging obedience, but Jonah is only doing this now out of obligation. His heart attitude hasn't been reconciled.
- He spent a very long time dwelling on his feelings as he walked to Nineveh. That month-long walk with few distractions, no amusements, and an unpleasant task at the end of it (as Jonah sees it) has given him much time for reflection.

    Isolation can prompt a time of self-reflection and meditation that brings positive heart change, but if the heart is in rebellion, that isolation can provide a very fertile environment for anger and resentment to grow. Anger steals our quiet time if we let it.
- When Jonah gets to Nineveh, he's geared up for a fight, and then the Ninevites repent. He wants the fight, but they won't fight back. So this leaves him with all this pent-up emotion.

Divine Irony

On the boat, God drove home that point that Jonah was no better than the heathen sailors. Now Jonah is in Nineveh, and he isn't any better than the Ninevites. There is violence in him. He wants the full force of God's wrath to fall on these heathen Ninevites and will rejoice to see it happen. The thought of that not happening sends him into a blinding rage.

The Ninevites are convicted over their violence. The King of Nineveh confesses that his people are a violent people. He exhorts them to put away violence from themselves, and the people are doing as they are told.

Yet here Jonah stands in their company—the one who is supposed to be God's ambassador—with this violent anger pent up inside him, aching for a fight, desiring the violence, and being denied it. Jonah listens to the King of Nineveh—his enemy—tell him and everyone else in nation to turn away from violence. I imagine Jonah thinks, "Who are these wretched heathen to be preaching to me about violence and evil?!"

Jonah is supposed to be an ambassador for God. He is the one who is supposed to have his act together and be the one to deal with the Ninevites' problem, but instead they are the ones working on him. How petty does it make God's ambassador look if he doesn't show at least as much restraint and repentance as these Ninevites? Perhaps we should ask why God's ambassador is the only one not convicted of his own problem. Does Jonah even recognize he has a problem?

Anger is a big stumbling block for us as ambassadors of God because it derails us from our purpose, and it blinds us to the lesson God is teaching us.

Sometimes God orchestrates sermons from the most unlikely places and from people whom we never thought we would take a lesson. And yet these words come out of their mouths and hit us in the heart, right where we are spiritually failing in that moment. God uses Kings of Nineveh to speak to us, too.

Jonah is at a breaking point.

How does Jonah deal with his anger?

> *"So he prayed to the LORD, and said, 'Ah, LORD, was not this what I said when I was still in my country? Therefore I fled previously to Tarshish; for I know that You are a gracious and merciful God, slow to anger and abundant in lovingkindness, One who relents from doing harm. Therefore now, O LORD, please take my life from me, for it is better for me to die than to live!'"—Jonah 4:2-3*

Jonah vents to God that he is still looking for an escape, even an escape into death. That is his way of coping with this. He says, "Have mercy on me and just kill me now." At least he has learned that he can't take his own life. God taught him that with the fish. Yet you can feel the anger and resentment toward God still building in Jonah.

That's the thing about emotions—good or bad, they have a lot of energy behind them, especially anger. Emotions fluctuate up and down, increasing and decreasing, but sometimes they grow to an extreme.

Jonah is building up to an extreme.

How Emotions Build

Positive emotions, like love and joy, build up and out. They begin within us and build outward toward others.

Negative emotions are at the other end of the spectrum. They also begin within us, but build in a downward and increasingly inward direction. They make us more and more withdrawn and self-focused.

There are three big classes of negative emotions: anger, fear, and sorrow. This is how each builds:

- **Anger**: Begins with an irritation, and progresses to agitation, which escalates to violence. In its extremity, it ends in murder—taking the life of another person.
- **Fear**: Begins with guilt, and progresses to worry, which escalates to anxiety. In its extremity, it ends in paranoia—thinking someone else will take your life.
- **Sorrow**: Begins with discontent, and progresses to depression, which escalates to despair. In its extremity, it ends in suicide—taking your own life.

In their extremities, all negative emotions end in death. What's more, when you get to the extreme level, all begin to merge and transfer from one to another. Murder is often followed by suicide. Paranoia can drive a person to murder and/or take their own life. When you get into the realm of death, all these negative emotions get muddled.

God's prophets end up in these extremes more often than we realize. When God uses them, He takes them to extremes, but then He is very compassionate in dealing with them at that point and in bringing them back from that brink.

Jonah is already at the extreme. He is so angry he wants to murder, and being restrained, he pleads for death.

We see the same pattern in Elijah (1 Kings 19:1-4) after he executed Jezebel's wicked prophets. He hit that high level of emotion in taking life. Then he ran for his life in fear of Jezebel, thinking he was the only prophet of God left in the world (paranoia) and then depression took hold and he begged God to take his life.

Though not a prophet per se, Cain displayed the same pattern. He was the first man in the history of humankind to get angry, and he didn't know how to handle it. His anger escalated to murder, crossed over to fear of being killed, and then again to depression over being sent out of God's presence.

Among the three negative emotions, anger is unique in how it builds.

- **Anger has a memory.** That is where anger gets its energy from—the memories. You get angry the first time, that memory goes into you, and you hold onto it. The next time a similar incident happens, you remember the first time and add that level of anger to the second instance. Then you add both of those to the third time, and so anger builds by storing up memories. Whatever level of anger you get to the first time is the starting place for the next time.
- **Whatever level of anger you reach over one issue can transfer over to other issues.** A minor irritation may come up, let's say, over finding a red sock in a tub of white laundry. It is irritating to have to rewash an entire tub of laundry that has turned pink because of the red sock. Irritation is Level 1 anger. But if your anger is already at Level 20 toward the person who thoughtlessly put the tub of whites on to wash without checking for red socks, then you take that Level 20 anger and throw it on top of the sock issue. This is what happens to Jonah a few verses later over the issue of a vine that dies as a result of being eaten by a worm. Hang on to this thought.
- **Anger and mercy are at constant war with each other.** Anger wants to hold on to the memories; mercy requires you to let them go. God can't get Jonah to be merciful until He deals with the anger in Jonah.

Remember God's policy on mercy?

> "But if a wicked man turns from all his sins which he has committed, keeps all My statutes, and does what is lawful and right, he shall surely live; he shall not die. <u>None of the transgressions which he has committed shall be remembered against him</u>; because of the righteousness which he has done, he shall live." —Ezekiel 18:21-22 (emphasis added)

Jonah doesn't want to give up the memory of the Ninevites' offenses. He doesn't want to let go of his anger. His rage builds to the point of violence seeking an outlet. Extreme violence, being restrained, breaks to the other side of the spectrum, and Jonah seeks death, which is where he stays for the rest of the narrative.

Jonah's example is a warning to us. Deal with your anger before it has time to grow. Guard your thought life. If you find that your quiet moments are filled with thoughts of anger or frustration with a person, go to that person and work through the issue. Get a counselor to help you if you can't reconcile on your own. Don't let those feelings of anger build. Unresolved anger can be such a roadblock in our spiritual growth. We must be willing to give up the memory of the offense and the anger that goes with it.

A Fine and Pleasant Misery

> *(Jonah 4:3, paraphrase) "Since you are such a merciful God, have mercy on me and take my life. It would be a fine and pleasant thing if I could just die now."*

Jonah gets a little sarcastic with God at this point. He is up in God's face about this, because God is bringing to light a whole lot of emotions and issues that are excruciating to face. Jonah twists and turns under that microscope of self-examination and seeks an escape.

Out of His mercy and compassion, God willingly wrestles with Jonah even though God has every right to blast him. God restrains Himself and simply asks a question that goes straight to the heart of the issue.

> *"Is it right for you to be angry?"—Jonah 4:4*
> *Alternate versions: "Do you have good reason to be angry?"*

Isn't it infuriating when you have all this pent-up emotion, and you are venting to a person, only to have that person look at you calmly and ask this kind of rational, philosophical question—as if we are thinking rationally in that moment? Our rational mind knows we shouldn't be angry about whatever the issue is, but we are. We shouldn't be angry when the worst sinner gets saved. We should be joyful to have a relationship with such a merciful God.

But logic isn't driving us at this moment. Emotions are.

The Hebrew word for "right" means to do well. This is something along the lines of what God said to Cain when He rejected Cain's sacrifice.

> *"So the LORD said to Cain, 'Why are you angry? And why has your countenance fallen? If you do well, will you not be accepted? And if you do not do well, sin lies at the door. And its desire is for you, but you should rule over it.'"—Genesis 4:6-7*

The same Hebrew word also means contented or happy, to be glad. This adds a deeper nuance to that question as it appeals to emotions. "Is it good for you to be angry?" "Are you pleased to be angry?" "Are you content being angry?" There is a subtle hint that we should consider what effect anger is having on our well-being. Have we ever met someone who isn't happy unless they are angry about something or have something to complain about? Someone who isn't happy unless they are miserable? Don't we just want to ask them, "Are you happy being angry?"

Why doesn't Jonah want to answer the question? Why wouldn't we want to answer that question?

Because to answer that question, we would have to admit that anger is eating us up. When we let this anger rule us for so long, it becomes a part of who we are. It defines us. We are miserable, and in truth, we are hurting ourselves by allowing it to consume us.

There are some questions we just don't want to answer because they are painful to deal with—they unravel you emotionally, and make us feel very vulnerable.

Jonah sits in the middle of his ISIS camp and has a spiritual meltdown. If we were Jonah, the last thing we would want is to be made emotionally vulnerable in the presence of our enemies—people we don't trust, who might hurt us. If we had to explain our anger, then we would have to admit how we feel about them, how we want God's wrath to fall on them, and it would be like being back on trial in front of the heathen sailors all over again. Jonah's anger brings him back to that dilemma.

But this time Jonah is not stuck on a boat in the middle of the sea.

He doesn't want to answer that question. He doesn't want to think about it or talk about it. So he turns and walks out of the city. He walks away from the Ninevites and away from God. Again.

Happiness is a Sukkah

> *"So Jonah went out of the city and sat on the east side of the city. There he made himself a shelter and sat under it in the shade, till he might see what would become of the city." —Jonah 4:5*

Jonah heads out of the city to the east. Heading east in the Scripture usually indicates heading away from God and deeper into sin. I think he is leaving the city for a few reasons:

- He walks away from Nineveh to get away from the conviction he feels there.
- He feels he has completed his obligation. The first time, he walks away

without paying his vows to God. Now that his obligation is fulfilled, he walks away again. His mission to deliver God's message is done. God never said anything about sticking around to disciple this bunch of believing heathen. It isn't part of his contract. Right?

- He still secretly hopes for God's wrath to fall on Nineveh; and if it does, he doesn't want to be in the city when it happens. He doesn't want that judgment falling on him, too. After all, he is not one of them. Right?

Again, Jonah goes out of the presence of the Lord and makes another little nest for himself in a place where he shouldn't be. It isn't as nice of a nest as the one that he made in the ship's hold among all those luxury items. He's not sleeping on Egyptian linens and cotton bales this time. This is a *sukkah*—a rough little booth improvised from whatever materials are at hand. A *sukkah* is not very comfortable apart from offering scant shade, but it is the best he can do for himself (and maybe it suits his mood). Jonah sits in his booth and waits to see what happens to Nineveh.

God is still pursuing Jonah, faithfully, kindly, with great patience and great persistence. Instead of waiting for Jonah to return to Him this time, God seeks him out. God comes to Jonah and meets him where he is. God sees him sitting under his crude little shelter and decides to make Jonah's nest a little more comfortable.

> "And the LORD God prepared a plant and made it come up over Jonah, that it might be shade for his head to deliver him from his misery. So Jonah was very grateful for the plant." —Jonah 4:6

It is a testament to God's love and mercy that He causes a vine to grow up over the shelter so that it is cool and shady for Jonah. What God provides for him is ever so much better than what he could provide for himself. And now Jonah is very happy. Again, the English translation is a little tame. The NKJV translates it as "grateful." The NASB says Jonah was "extremely happy." The Hebrew word means "rejoicing with great joy."

Maybe Jonah rejoices for a couple reasons:

- First, it seems perhaps that God empathizes with Jonah. He comes out to Jonah, treats him kindly, and provides this shady plant which comforts him.
- There is also a little part of Jonah that rejoices because he has always been one to seek his own comfort. He loves comfortable living to whatever degree he can get it. It seems Jonah's happiness in life is defined by his comfortableness.

Remember the nest Jonah made for himself in the hold of the ship? No sooner had he settled into that comfortable place, than the sailors burst in, rousted him out of his cozy bed, and threw everything overboard into the sea. Just as quickly as Jonah's luxury bedding disappeared over the side of the ship, so his beautiful vine disappears.

God gives Jonah a brief respite before continuing the lesson on mercy. Now the lesson commences. Jonah is not where he is supposed to be, so God makes life uncomfortable for him.

> *"But as morning dawned the next day God prepared a worm, and it so damaged the plant that it withered. And it happened, when the sun arose, that God prepared a vehement east wind; and the sun beat on Jonah's head, so that he grew faint. Then he wished death for himself, and said, 'It is better for me to die than to live.'"—Jonah 4:7-8*

Compare this with Jonah's experience on the boat in the storm:

- In one day, all his comfort is destroyed. The fleeting things that bring him such happiness are gone. Again.
- Now the east wind is blowing in his life. Again.
- A storm rages inside him. Again.
- He becomes faint, at the end of his strength. Again. (Remember Jonah 2:7.)
- He wants to die. Again.

It is the same lesson, just with different people, in different places, under different circumstances. Jonah's behavior remains the same, as have the consequences.

Let's consider some of the symbolism in the plant and the worm. If the beautiful vine is Jonah, what is the worm eating him up inside?

> *"Then God said to Jonah, 'Is it right for you to be angry about the plant?' And he said, 'It is right for me to be angry, even to death!'" —Jonah 4:9*

I can just imagine Jonah saying: You want to talk about the plant, let's talk about the plant. Let's talk about how You came to me, gave me some sympathy and comfort, made that wonderful plant grow, and then the very next day, You took it away. Now I am hot, the wind is blowing me around, and I'm miserable again. Let's talk about what a merciful God You really are. Thanks for nothing.

It's just another reason to be angry, and another effort to hold on to that anger.

Jonah 4: Jonah and God, Again

All the anger Jonah has been building up toward God now gets transferred to the issue with the plant, and his anger is completely out of proportion. God let's the force of Jonah's emotions carry him to this extreme, and now He uses Jonah's anger to make His point about Jonah's lack of mercy.

> "But the LORD said, 'You have had pity on the plant for which you have not labored, nor made it grow, which came up in a night and perished in a night. And should I not pity Nineveh, that great city, in which are more than one hundred and twenty thousand persons who cannot discern between their right hand and their left—and much livestock?'"
> —Jonah 4:10-11

God feels about the Ninevites dying in their sins the way Jonah feels about that plant. God brings Jonah to an extreme level of emotion so that, hopefully, he feels exactly the way God does. God makes a *kal va'chomer,* "light and heavy," comparison. If Jonah pities something as small as the life of a plant, why doesn't he pity something as big as a city full of people— more than 120,000 people of whom "cannot discern between their right hand and their left"? It may be talking about children who have not yet reached the age of understanding, or it may be speaking of people who are childlike in their understanding of God. God points out the gross error in Jonah's priorities: "You pity a soulless plant that died in a day, yet you are angry with me for pitying a city full of people who are going to die in their sins, be judged righteously, and live for all eternity in hell?"

Jonah feels sorry for this plant that died when, in fact, he did nothing for it. He took the benefit from it, but did nothing to help it grow. He did nothing to stop the worm from eating it. It came up in a night and perished in a night. It was a "son of the night"—that is the Hebrew phrase here.

From God's perspective, the Ninevites are "sons of the night."

Seeing Nineveh from God's Perspective

"Is it right for you to be angry . . ." God asks the same question twice—once in regards to the Ninevites (Jonah 4:4) and here in regards to this plant (Jonah 4:9). When you see that kind of repetition in a passage, it is a cue that God wants us to consider the relationship between the two.

God compares Nineveh to a plant that flourishes only for a day. When God looks at people, He sees not just individuals but nations in a corporate sense. He doesn't just see this one generation, but the full extent of their existence as a people.

God has seen the Ninevites from their beginning in Genesis, and watched them grow as a nation. He sees them here at their low point, and extends mercy to this particular generation. He will bless them, and overnight they will grow and flourish for their day. Like that vine, the Assyrian nation will spread to cover the land, including Israel. It will become a mighty kingdom and world empire, and He will use them to accomplish His purpose in disciplining disobedient Israel (just as He uses this plant to discipline Jonah).

But in the end, the old evil will return and eat away at them like that worm, and Assyria will begin to wither and die, almost overnight. Then the Lord's judgment—that east wind—will blow on them and they will be swept away.

Jonah only sees the Ninevites of this one generation, and doesn't look beyond the moment. God sees the end of their empire as if it were tomorrow. They are only flourishing in this eleventh hour of their existence as a nation. In less than 200 years, they will be swallowed by the Babylonian Empire and disappear. Two hundred years is like tomorrow to God.

God tries to get Jonah to see the grand plan, to take the long view. He wants him to look beyond this generation to the next that will have such an impact on Israel, and even see the end of all generations and the judgment that is coming for everyone, ourselves included. He wants His ambassadors to see the end of all things as if it were happening tomorrow. Time is so short.

The text talks about 120,000 people *"who cannot discern between their right hand or their left."* They lack discernment, not knowing right from left, perhaps right from wrong. Remember, we are living in Old Testament times, so the Law is still in effect and the only way for a person to have a relationship with God. How are these Ninevites going to turn from their ways if they don't know what to do or what right living is supposed to be?

Is it enough to just throw the salvation message at people and then walk away? Is that where our obligation to God ends?

Applications

What brings you joy in life?

How does God shift His ambassadors out of their comfort zones?

Are anger, fear, or sorrow building in your life?

How do you deal with emotions that are hindering your work for God?

Have you recognized a behavior pattern in your life that needs changing? If so, describe it.

How did God impress on you the need to change that behavior pattern?

Jewish Application of Jonah

FROM THE EYES OF JESUS' DISCIPLES

Before we move on to Part 2 and the pictures of Christ in Jonah, I think it would be helpful to explain where the book of Jonah fits in context with Jewish worship practices and thinking. Jewish worship has changed tremendously over the years and without the Temple, few sects follow even a semblance of the orthodox practices that Jesus and His disciples lived by; so what I explain here is not something you may see in modern synagogues. I attempt to present the more traditional Jewish understanding and application of the book of Jonah as it might have been applied in the days of the Second Temple.

This information has been gleaned from orthodox Jewish teachings and commentaries, and is supported by the pictures we have of Jewish practices in the Gospels. My intent is to help you understand how the book of Jonah would have been incorporated into Jewish life in the days of Jesus and His disciples and why Jesus used Jonah as an example to the Pharisees who had become increasingly corrupt and unrepentant.

Jonah and the Day of Atonement

Jewish lifestyle, then and now, revolves around the yearly feasts. While the Temple was standing, there were three yearly pilgrimmage feasts where all Jewish men had to present themselves at the Temple in Jerusalem. Even though the Temple is no longer standing, many orthodox men still make the trips to Jerusalem each year. In addition to physical travel, several of the feasts require a good deal of physical planning and preparation beforehand as they are week-long feasts.

The Day of Atonement ("Yom Kippur") is one of the festivals that requires a good deal of preparation spiritually, as it is the day traditionally appointed for Israel to present itself before God and have atonement made for the nation. In Temple times, it was the one day each year when the High Priest was allowed to go behind the veil into the Holy of Holies with the incense and the blood offering to make atonement for the people. It was the day when the two goats—the sacrifice and the scapegoat—were offered before the Lord as covering for the sins of the people. It was a day of judgment for Israel, but also a day when they would be forgiven by God and reconciled to Him—a time of mourning turned to joy.

Even though the Temple and priesthood have been removed, and the sacrificial system no longer followed, the Day of Atonement remains for the Jewish people a time of considering Who God is and who they are, and what their purpose was and still is in this world. It is a time of self-assessment of their relationship with God and with the people around them. The themes of Jonah are very fitting to this solemn festival.

In Jesus' day, when coming to the judgment on the Day of Atonement, you would not appear before the Lord without having examined yourself, turned away from sin in your life, and made some effort to reconcile yourself with those you had wronged. Thus, preparation for this day would traditionally begin 40 days ahead of time. The priests and rabbis would begin a series of special Scripture readings meant to prompt the people to examine their lives, their relationships with others and with God, and to repent of their sins. These forty days are appropriately called the "Season of Teshuvah" (Season of Repentance). Of those forty days, the last ten, called the Days of Awe, are considered a time of intense divine scrutiny and heart testing to see if the person should be counted righteous and written in the Book of Life, or wicked and written in the Book of Death. According to Jewish tradition, the Lord's judgment on the Day of Atonement seals the fate of the righteous and wicked.[1]

The Day of Atonement is observed with fasting, prayer, and repentance—all themes that we find in the book of Jonah. The forty days of the Ninevite's testing, the sincerity of their fasting and prayer, followed by God's mercy on them—all go hand-in-hand with the repentance prescribed for the Day of Atonement. For this reason, the book of Jonah is the special reading for this festival as it reinforces the heart and understanding of it.

According to Jewish tradition, there are several reasons why Jonah is read on the Day of Atonement.[2]

1) To remind God's people of His infinite mercy. If He could forgive the Ninevites their great sin, then there is hope for forgiveness to be offered to His people.

2) To remind God's people of the model of repentance in the Ninevites' example.

---

[1] Parsons, John J. "Yom Kippur–Day of Atonement." *Hebrew for Christians*, www.hebrew4christians.com/Holidays/Fall_Holidays/Yom_Kippur/yom_kippur.html (Accessed December 28, 2018).

[2] Bernstein, Maya "Jonah and Yom Kippur." *My Jewish Learning*, https://www.myjewishlearning.com/article/jonah-yom-kippur/ (Accessed December 28, 2018).

3) To remind God's people that all creation is in God's hands—as shown by His preparing the storm, the fish, the plant, and the worm—and that the lives of all men and animals are precious to Him.

Notice how the focus is more on the Ninevites' example than Jonah's. Why would the Ninevites be a better example of repentance than God's own prophet? We will discuss that shortly, but first let's define the act of repentance, according to Jewish interpretation and practice.

Repentance in Jewish Practice (Ideally)

Teshuvah is the word the Jews use to describe repentance. It comes from the word, *shuv*, meaning to return. The Jewish definition of repentance is the act of turning—changing your mind, changing your path in life—and returning to righteous living. It includes confession but entails more than that in Jewish thought.

Teshuvah was made at both the individual and national levels for Israel. Without a Temple today, the focus has shifted away from national atonement and more toward atoning for the individual's responsibility. There are some basic steps for repentance which I have gleaned from a number of Jewish sources and explained here. We, as Christians, should recognize these, as they are the same pattern of self-examination we practice, or ought to practice, before partaking of communion.

1) Recognize the sin. You cannot turn from sin unless you first identify it in your life. This requires spending time in reflection and self-evaluation.

2) Renounce the sin (put away the sin, stop doing it). You admit to yourself that the action is wrong and stop doing it. You have to stop doing it before you confess it. For instance, you cannot confess an adulterous affair if you are still participating in the adulterous affair.

3) Confess the sin. You publicly admit that the action is wrong. This means you go to the person(s) you wronged and confess your sin to them. Additionally, you go to people besides the ones you wronged if your sin also affected them, and confess your sin to them. If your family is struggling because of some sin you committed, you confess the sin to your spouse first, and then you apologize to your children and extended family if they, too, are affected.

4) Reconcile with the person you have wronged. There could be some serious emotional fallout as a result of your confession. You may need to spend some significant time talking it out, giving the person(s) you wronged some time to sort out their feelings. According to Jewish practice, you must have their acknowledged verbal forgiveness before the Day of Atonement.

Being forgiven and restored on the Day of Atonement didn't just rely on being forgiven by God. It required being forgiven by others first. God would not accept someone who hadn't reconciled or at least attempted to reconcile with his brother. How much different would our spiritual lives be if we thought God would not forgive us unless the people in our lives had forgiven us first?

In this study of Jonah, we talk about being on both sides of mercy:

- Being merciful to someone over whom you have the power to hurt.
- Being at the mercy of someone who has the power to hurt you.

Under the Old Testament Law, a lack of forgiveness could hurt someone in a way that had eternal consequences:

- If a person repents and you refuse to forgive them, you are, in essence, cutting them off from God.
- If you repent and they refuse to forgive you, then you could be cut off from God.

This seems extreme, and yet it should not be a foreign concept to us. Jesus taught this in His Sermon on the Mount.

> "Therefore if you bring your gift to the altar, and there remember that your brother has something against you, leave your gift there before the altar, and go your way. First be reconciled to your brother, and then come and offer your gift."— Matthew 5:23-24

> "... forgive us our debts, as we forgive our debtors."—Matthew 6:12

> "For if you forgive men their trespasses, your heavenly Father will also forgive you. But if you do not forgive men their trespasses, neither will your Father forgive your trespasses."—Matthew 6:14-15

> "So My heavenly Father also will do to you if each of you, from his heart, does not forgive his brother his trespasses."—Matthew 18:35

Many of Jesus' parables give the example of a person who was forgiven a debt, but refuses to forgive a brother who owes them a debt. As a result, mercy was taken away from the unforgiving servant and punishment is given instead. These are Day-of-Atonement type of messages.

Sadly, today, it is a fact that there are people in our lives who will never forgive us for our sins, no matter how repentant we are or how much we change our lives. They carry the anger and the grudge against us perpetually, and we, in truth, do the same to others. In this we are very much like Jonah.

Thankfully, because of our relationship with Christ, our relationship with God is not in jeopardy the way it was under the Old Testament Law. Yet we live with the brokenness that comes from a lack of forgiveness—a brokenness that God never wants to be part of our lives—and we contribute to the brokenness in other people's lives when we do not forgive. If someone comes to you seeking forgiveness, don't add to their brokenness by not forgiving them. Forgiveness is an act of mercy to which God calls all of us.

Under Old Testament law, since obtaining someone's forgiveness was required for atonement to be accepted, there was a rule made in Judaism that if someone came to you multiple times asking for forgiveness, on the third time, you were required to grant forgiveness if their repentance was sincere and they had taken steps to make amends.

5) Make restitution. There is a long list of sins for which Mosaic Law required restitution in various forms; and if we were under the Law, we would have to make restitution, in addition to offering sacrifices. For instance, corrupt tax collectors would have to return all the money they extorted from people with 20% added as a fine. In Luke 19, after Zacchaeus the tax collector has a change of heart, he promises to give half his goods to the poor and returns the money he had extorted fourfold. That is an act of *teshuvah*.

But what if you owe more than you can pay back? Imagine if you were Jonah and had to pay the sailors for the cost of the luxury cargo that was thrown into the sea on account of your disobedience to God? Or had to reimburse them for years of lost income? Or had to pay for damages to the ship? If that is the case, then you cast yourself on the mercy of the King, but you better release everyone else from their debts to you as well. A number of Jesus' parables set up this scenario.

But restitution doesn't end with just the reimbursement for property. If part of the reconciliation and recovery process requires counseling or therapy for the victim, then making amends can also include financial compensation for these things as well. If you cause damage, whether physically, psychologically, or emotionally, then you pay for the repair—not just of the property, but of the person.

6) Resolve not to do the sin again. You turn from the sin, and act in a way that is opposite of the sin. If you stole, then give back. If you lied, then tell the truth. There should be a change of heart here, but it doesn't necessarily happen, as we see in Jonah's case. There can be just a change of behavior without a change of heart.

If a Jewish person is truly sincere, he might also perform a *mikveh*—an act of bodily immersion in a bath of water. I explain this practice more in Part 2, but I mention it here as a practice associated with the Day of Atonement and repentance. Being immersed and then drawn out of the water is likened to becoming a new person, putting the old sin behind you, and starting over with a clean slate. It is meant as a public testimony of a person's intention to repent.

When all this is accomplished, only then would you:

7) Go to God, and confess the sin (and take your sacrifice).

The repentance process can take a long time, and the Jewish people had a deadline of the 10th day of the 7th month to accomplish it.

On the actual Day of Atonement, the people fast in accordance with the Law to *"afflict your soul."* As part of the corporate expression of repentance, the entire congregation recites a formal prayer of confession called the *Al Chet*, a lengthy list of 44 sins that covers just about everything. As each sin was recited, the repentant person would knock his chest with his fist (as described in Luke 18:13).

Everyone recited the whole list, whether they were guilty of all those things or not, because in Jewish thought, we are responsible to a certain extent for the sin of our brother. This comes from Levitcus 19:17:

> "You shall not hate your brother in your heart. You shall surely rebuke your neighbor, and not bear sin because of him."

If one Jew saw another Jew transgressing the Law and failed to rebuke him—if he made no effort to warn him and help him maintain purity and holiness before the Lord—then both would be considered guilty of the same sin. Failure to rebuke was equated to hating your brother. This is why the self-righteous Pharisees were so diligent in pointing out other people's transgressions of the Law, because they would have incurred guilt themselves otherwise. In their hearts, they felt they were being righteous, perhaps even zealous, by making sure everyone else knew their sin, so that they themselves would not bear any guilt on account of another person.

In that simple illustration, you can see what is very wrong with the heart attitudes of many of the Jewish leaders of Jesus' day, and you can see the same lack of heart demonstrated in Jonah, who repents according to the letter of the Law but not in his own spirit. You can approach the keeping of these laws from one of two hearts:

- One heart has genuine care for a sinning brother. If done correctly, rebuking someone can be an act of love when you seek to turn him from a particular sin in his life. He may not listen to you or turn from his sin, but you make the effort for his sake and do it in a loving way out of care for him as a brother. That is why Leviticus 19:17 begins with the statement about not hating your brother. Loving your brother must come first and is the right heart behind the act of rebuke. Get your heart right before you judge your brother—pick the plank out of your own eye before you go after the speck in theirs (see the Sermon on the Mount, Matthew 7:1-5)
- The other is the heart of a Pharisee, who doesn't care about the brother at all but only about the guilt he himself incurs if he doesn't speak up. He considers it his *obligation* before God to speak up, regardless of how he feels toward the brother—if he even considers him to be a brother.

It is almost as if the Pharisees broke Levitcus 19:17 apart and treated each part separately. Loving your brother was one issue, and rebuking people of sin was another issue. By removing the command to love from the equation, rebuking a person could be done without any feeling toward them, one way or another. As long as you rebuked them, you felt very self-righteous for having kept your obligation to the Law and not incurred sin.

Loving your brother became something that had to be defined, because you had an obligation to seek the well-being of a brother, but not the well-being of an enemy (a Pharisaical teaching derived from Deuteronomy 23:6). Some wretched sinner like a tax collector or harlot would never be considered a brother, so it would not be a sin if you didn't seek their well-being. How much more so a Ninevite?

We see this play out in Jonah. Perhaps Jonah did not confess the sins against the sailors, or even his wrong heart toward the Ninevites because he did not classify them as brothers; therefore, he might hate the Ninevites and not seek the sailors' well-being without thinking it a sin.

This is the same attitude that leads to Jesus' parable of the Pharisee and the Tax Collector.

> *"Also He* [Jesus] *spoke this parable to some who trusted in themselves that they were righteous, and despised others: 'Two men went up to the temple to pray, one a Pharisee and the other a tax collector. The Pharisee*

Jewish Application of Jonah | 95

stood and prayed thus with himself, "God, I thank You that I am not like other men—extortioners, unjust, adulterers, or even as this tax collector. I fast twice a week; I give tithes of all that I possess." And the tax collector, standing afar off, would not so much as raise his eyes to heaven, but beat his breast, saying, "God, be merciful to me a sinner!" I tell you, this man went down to his house justified rather than the other; for everyone who exalts himself will be humbled, and he who humbles himself will be exalted.'"—Luke 18:9-14

In this illustration, the Pharisee—who should model repentance for the people—is the worse of the two examples, while the tax collector's repentance is found more acceptable. The same contrast is seen when comparing Jonah with the Ninevites. In studying Jonah 2, we critiqued Jonah's prayer of repentance, what he said and didn't say, and find that his turning is more of a response out of obligation than a desire to see the Ninevites reconciled with God. Let's compare Jonah's response to the Ninevites in Jonah 3.

Repentance: Jonah vs. the Ninevites

- In both cases, there is a response of fasting. The Ninevites' fasting is voluntary. They choose to fast out of a heart response to God, whereas Jonah's fast is out of sheer necessity, not wanting to eat anything that washed into the belly of that fish.
- Both men and beasts of Nineveh go into mourning over their sin before the Lord. The King of Nineveh identifies very clearly what is the sin of the people, and exhorts them to turn. After all Jonah's failure as an ambassador for God and his unmerciful treatment of the sailors, his only show of remorse is a pricking of conscience over some vows. Looking at the steps of repentance, his prayer lacks remorse and confession, not to mention restitution for the loss his sin caused others.
- The King of Nineveh rebukes his people out of a desire to save them, whereas Jonah rebukes them out of a desire for their judgment.
- The Ninevites, led by the King of Nineveh, react spontaneously in true repentance and turn from their ways voluntarily. Jonah's turning is done out of obligation, without any change in heart attitude.

Of the two, the Ninevites of this generation actually prove to be a better model of repentance than this rebellious son of Israel. This generation of

Ninevites claims distinction as the role model to which Jesus points when rebuking the rebellious sons of Israel in His day.

> *"The men of Nineveh will rise up in the judgment with this generation and condemn it, because they repented at the preaching of Jonah; and indeed a greater than Jonah is here."—Matthew 12:41*

I think it is interesting how Jesus' use of the Ninevites' example for the lesson is consistent with even modern-day rabbis' application of the book of Jonah. I almost wonder if the Day of Atonement isn't the setting for this passage in Matthew, as it certainly follows the context of the festival.

For Reflection

It can be an agonizing task coming to terms with our true selves and our identity and responsibility that are part of our relationship with God. We can spend a lot of time immersed in the distractions of this world to avoid facing the truth about ourselves. Yet we must do this, and it is better to do it voluntarily before the storm of consequences engulfs us. If there is one message that springs from Jonah, (and is very much the heart of the Day of Atonement), it is that there is infinite mercy and forgiveness for those who return to God.

Whether you are preparing for Yom Kippur or taking communion, consider the steps of repentance listed here. Turn out your spiritual cupboards and consider the relationships in your life. Don't think just about your sins against God, but your sins against people who have been impacted, perhaps for the worse, by your words and actions. Have you kept your word to do what you said you would do to set things right? Are you fighting God's calling in your life? Do not treat this lightly.

The Earthen Vessel

SUMMARY

The book of Jonah ends abruptly with God's final word on the subject of Nineveh. We don't see Jonah's response to see if he is convicted and has a haphak-ing moment of his own. It may be that this prophet from the northern kingdom of Israel becomes the first of that nation to enter exile and die in Assyria. There is no indication that he ever returns to Israel.

And so we are left with this unresolved picture of Jonah. He is the epitome of the earthen vessel with all the flaws endemic to the character of such base clay—flaws that even a stint in the belly of the fish could not completely purge from him. He remains brittle and unyielding to the end.

Character Sketch of an Earthen Vessel

Jonah's character is a caricature of the lowly, flawed earthen vessel. He is God's unwilling ambassador to the Gentile nations, who struggles with:

- following God's will and calling in his life
- seeing people the way God sees them
- seeing value in those who live in wicked and repulsive lifestyles
- being merciful to these people the way God desires to be merciful to them—not just out of obligation, but out of a true heart desire to see them saved.

Selfish, self-focused, self-righteous Jonah struggles with anger, prejudice, and hate; yet he sees himself as being zealous for the Lord in hating the things that the Lord hates. He is blind to his own condition, claiming a relationship with God the Creator yet denying God's sovereignty over his life. He is determined to follow his own path, even when it takes him downward into the darkest of places. He is prone to making nests for himself in places where he shouldn't be, and has to be rousted out of his comfort zone time and again. His disobedience brings storms into people's lives, but he doesn't care what damage he causes.

He doesn't care about saving unbelievers because he himself doesn't appreciate what it truly means to be separated from God until God puts him through those lessons—and Jonah has to go through those same lessons repeatedly.

Yet, when Jonah is at his very worst and all his character flaws are on full display both physically and spiritually, we look at him and think he must be the worst example of everything a son of the kingdom should be; yet this is when God writes His own story in all its glory into the narrative of Jonah's life. In Part 2, I will show you the story of Jesus Christ in glorious detail through the book of Jonah.

Self-Assessment for Earthen Vessels

We may not have reached the extremes that Jonah experienced, but all of us should be able to relate to aspects of Jonah's struggle. As earthen vessels ourselves, perhaps we should rate our overall level of mercy.

How good are you at being God's ambassador?

Do people see God's mercy when they look at you?

Do you want to see people saved, even people like ISIS terrorists?

What is an example of how you have exercised mercy?

Have you ever performed an act of mercy that involved a personal sacrifice? If so, what did you have to sacrifice?

How merciful are you when delivering a difficult or rebuking message?

Has God put a burden on your heart to go to someone, and you are resisting? If so, why are you resisting?

When God puts burdens on our hearts to go to someone, we need to go. Even if we think these people will never change. Even if they are our enemies. We never know how God has been working in their lives to prepare them for a relationship with Himself.

This wraps up Part 1 and our examination of the earthen vessel. In Part 2 we see how God fills that vessel with His glory.

PART TWO

The Glory of God in the Earthen Vessel

INTRODUCTION

Seeing the Picture within the Picture

We are now going to make a second pass through the book of Jonah so that I can show you the pictures of Christ within the narrative. To do this we need to change how we study the text.

So far, we have worked straight through the text, verse by verse, in a very linear fashion which is a good exegetical practice. But this approach doesn't bring out the picture of Christ with nearly as much clarity. To find the picture within the picture, we have to tackle the text in a more spatial fashion.

Putting Together the Jigsaw Puzzle

Consider the book of Jonah a jigsaw puzzle, and its verses, the puzzle pieces. There is a somewhat universal strategy for putting together a puzzle.

1) **Know what end picture we are building toward.** In our case, the end picture is the life of Christ. We have the benefit of knowing the end picture, but the Jewish people didn't. They had to build this picture without a reference.

2) **Find the edges and put those together to establish the frame.** When God gave Israel this Old Testament puzzle, He didn't give them any edge pieces except the first edge—all the "first" things. From there the Old Testament picture builds out in all directions. Israel had to follow the picture as it built through the narrative, not knowing how far it would go or if they had reached the end of the picture. We will do the same. Jonah is one of those books that leaves the picture without a defined beginning or conclusion. It is simply a small picture floating within the much bigger picture of Christ in the Old Testament. So, we have no other edges to frame the picture, but at least we know toward what end we are building.

3) **Identify the pieces and begin building small parts of the picture.** To do this, we need to boil down the narrative of Jonah into very basic who-what-when-where elements—the characters, things, times, places, events, and basic actions. Then we gather together

other Old Testament verses related to each element and build a small picture around it. For instance, Jonah rejoices under a plant-shaded booth. The booth is an element that is found in other places in the Old Testament, so we incorporate those additional references to our understanding of the booth in its Jonah context. Thus we draw a general understanding from the small pictures of what each element, like the booth, signifies in Scripture and then apply that to the picture of Christ.

This may seem like a laborious task, but it is vital because these small pictures gathered around words and phrases become building blocks for the bigger picture of Christ. Building a picture library out of the Old Testament helps not only with our study of Jonah but also with our study of the Old Testament overall. The building blocks we put together here are the same building blocks used in other Old Testament books to build the picture of Christ.

4) Put the small pictures together to create one large picture.
As we begin to build the picture of Christ out of Jonah, we won't be building the larger picture straight through the narrative from the first to last verse in a linear fashion. That would be like trying to put a jigsaw puzzle together by building one straight line of pieces from left to right—it doesn't work. Instead we will work through the passages in chunks, putting together different combinations of building blocks to create different aspects of Christ's life.

For instance, let's say Jonah 1-3 contains building blocks 1–10. These passages contain two pictures of Christ: His physical baptism at the beginning of His ministry and His death (which He described as a baptism). You have to use building blocks 1, 2, 3, and 8 to build the picture of His physical baptism, but you have to use building blocks 2, 3, 6, 8, and 10 to build the picture of His death. There are elements that both pictures share, but then each picture has elements specific to it.

As we go through this, I hope you begin to understand why the Jewish people had difficulty sorting out the pictures of Christ. If you aren't given the final picture of Christ to know what you are looking for, it can be hard to determine which set of blocks to combine together into a picture, especially where small pictures overlap.

So, in short, this is what we will do for this part of the study:

1) Deconstruct the narrative into its basic elements—who, what, when, where, and basic actions.

2) Build small piles of knowledge and a general summary around each element to create a set of picture-building blocks.

3) Work back through the narrative of Jonah using our building blocks to reconstruct a picture of Christ.

Deconstructing Jonah

Find the Narrative Elements (people, places, things, times)

A high level overview gives us these basic narrative elements:

1) God
2) Jonah
3) Great (East) wind
4) Ship
5) Sailors
6) Sea
7) A great fish
8) Ninevites
9) King of Nineveh
10) Three days
11) The third day
12) A passage through water
13) A branch-covered booth
14) A worm

Create a Pile of Knowledge Around Each Element

Some of these elements are fairly straight forward, but some have more context to add to the picture when we examine where else they are found in Scripture.

To build a picture around them, we need the help of a concordance. I like to use the online concordance found at *www.blueletterbible.org* to find the Hebrew word behind the English translation and then search for that Hebrew word in the Old Testament text.

As you gather the associated verses, note the context of the additional verses. Does the word or phrase mean the same in those contexts as it does in the Jonah context? If it means something different, then consider what additional understanding might be contributed to the Jonah context.

This is actually a very Jewish way to study the Old Testament, and what you get at the end of the exercise is a vast library of types. We study types as part of New Testament Bible study, but those types usually center on the figure of Christ, and even then we only study the really obvious Old Testament examples. Jewish scholars, however, get to a whole new depth of imagery. So, in this chapter, we are going deeper with them. I am going to show you how to build a library of types; and in the next chapter, I will show you how to apply that library.

As we work through the elements, test how much you already know about the pictures they present in Scripture.

GOD

God is God. There is no defining the "Who-what-when-where" of Him, so we will leave Him as His own building block element, but note that His actions in the narrative include:

- Hurling down a storm
- Calming the sea
- Preparing a fish
- Causing the fish to deliver Jonah back to land
- Relenting in judgment
- Confronting Jonah
- Preparing a vine
- Preparing a worm
- Preparing an east wind

JONAH

Jonah is a complex building block that has a sub-element as part of his picture. The simple who-what-when-where details we know about Jonah are that he is:

- A Hebrew man from the northern kingdom of Israel
- A prophet
- A *tsiyr* (bringer of bad news, yet bringer of health)
- Associated with a passage through water (baptism)
- His name means "dove." Any time God calls a person by name for a particular purpose, you should look up the meaning of that name because it often adds to the context of the passage. The dove is an element on its own, so we will break that out separately.

Jonah's actions in this section include:

- Fleeing from God
- Sleeping through a storm
- Being put on trial
- Sacrificing himself to save others
- Being thrown over in judgment
- Going down into the sea
- Crying out to God
- Spending three days in the belly of the fish
- Repenting
- Being restored to land
- Prophesying in Nineveh
- Calling the people to be *haphak*-ed
- Getting angrier and angrier
- Building a booth
- Rejoicing under a plant-shaded booth
- Being left with a rebuke

DOVE

The name "Jonah" is the Hebrew word, *yownah*, which is the word for dove. The dove is a sub-element of Jonah and yet an element in its own right, and significant to the picture of Christ, so let's gather the contexts where that word appears:

- In the account of Noah and the dove (Genesis 8:8-12), the dove is a messenger sent over the waters that brings good news of new life.
- In Leviticus and Numbers, the dove is a sacrifice.
- In the Song of Songs, it is descriptive of the beauty of the Beloved, and a mate that is ever faithful.
- In the prophetic books (Isaiah, Jeremiah, Ezekiel, Hosea), the dove describes one who mourns and flaps about foolishly. Ezekiel and Hosea are particularly interesting in the picture they present:

    "Those who survive will escape and be on the mountains like doves of the valleys, all of them mourning, each for his iniquity."—Ezekiel 7:16

    "Ephraim also is like a silly dove, without sense—they call to Egypt, they go to Assyria. Wherever they go, I will spread My net on them; I will bring them down like birds of the air; I will chastise them according to what their congregation has heard."—Hosea 7:11-12

    "They shall come trembling like a bird from Egypt, like a dove from the land of Assyria. And I will let them dwell in their houses..."—Hosea 11:11

Let's come back to the Genesis 8:8-12 and look at Noah and the dove. Read that passage to yourself, only substitute the name "Jonah" wherever you see the word "dove."

What you get is this basic scenario: The *Jonah* is sent out the first time but doesn't accomplish the mission. It flaps around the sea for a while until finally being forced to return to Noah and is brought into the vessel of rescue. The *Jonah* is sent out again, this time with some success. The *Jonah* goes out a third time and does not return.

In the simplified version, you can see how close knit the scenarios of Jonah and Noah's dove are. Noah is to the dove as God is to Jonah.

There is a sub-picture attached to the dove in this account. In Genesis 8:9, the following phrase appears:

"the dove found <u>no resting place for the sole of her foot</u>." (emphasis added)

That phrase is repeated in Deuteronomy 28:65:

> "And among those nations you shall find no rest, <u>nor shall the sole of your foot have a resting place</u>; but there the LORD will give you a trembling heart, failing eyes, and anguish of soul." (emphasis added)

In this passage the Lord is speaking of disobedient Israel, likened to the dove, being exiled to the nations in a time of judgment. Jonah is the perfect representative of Israel in both his disobedience and experience as the dove "at sea" among the nations.

Summary of the dove picture:
- A messenger sent over the waters that brings good news of new life
- One who seeks a place to rest the sole of its foot
- Jonah, as the dove, is a messenger sent with a hard message
- A sacrifice
- One who mourns in iniquity
- One who flaps about foolishly
- Symbolic of disobedient Israel
- Symbolic of captives in Assyria

THE SHIP of TARSHISH

In Scripture, the ships of Tarshish are described as:
- Carriers of merchandise and luxury goods (1 Kings 10:11, 22; 2 Chronicles 9:21; Ezekiel 27:25-27)
- A source of perceived strength (Isaiah 23:1, 14, Isaiah 2:12-16)
- Broken by the east wind (Psalm 48:7)
- Saved by God in a time of storm (Psalm 107:21-31)
- In Jonah, the ship is a place of refuge being threatened in a hostile environment.

THE SEA

This is a very basic building block used to create some of the more complex pictures in Jonah. We will study its role more when we get to the third day and passages through water.
- A literal sea
- Figurative of Gentile nations, as opposed to Israel (the land)

GREAT WIND or EAST WIND

From what we know of this kind of storm, and the fact that it kept the sailors from returning to Israel, it is possible that the great wind in Jonah 1 was an east wind, which is an element repeated in Jonah 4.

The east wind is:

- Something that comes from God and can only be calmed by God.
- An agent of judgment. We see this in the following verses:
    - In Genesis 41:6, the east wind brings blight and famine.
    - In Exodus 10:13, it brings the locust plague on Egypt.
    - In Exodus 14:21, it swept back the waters of the Red Sea so Israel could cross but then the waters were released to overwhelm the Egyptians chasing them.
    - In Numbers 12 (cf Psalm 78:26), the Lord brings quail to the camp with an east wind as a test of Israel's faithfulness. The people's unrestrained pursuit of their cravings leads to their judgment.
    - It drives away the fool (Job 15:2), the rich man (Job 27:19-23), and the idolatrous and wicked (Jeremiah 18:17). These are all appropriate descriptions of Jonah. Consider the following verse in light of Jonah in the ship:

        "The rich man will lie down, but not be gathered up; He opens his eyes, and he is no more. Terrors overtake him like a flood; a tempest steals him away in the night. The east wind carries him away, and he is gone; it sweeps him out of his place. It hurls against him and does not spare; He flees desperately from its power. Men shall clap their hands at him, and shall hiss him out of his place."—Job 27:19-23

A GREAT FISH (VESSEL OF RESCUE)

The fish, as described in Jonah, is an anomaly in the Scripture; however, it is a type of what I would call a vessel of rescue in the role that it plays, similar to Noah's ark.

- Vessel of rescue

THE SAILORS

The sailors are localized to the book of Jonah, so we will simply summarize the picture of them from the narrative. A picture of Christ is going to incorporate some of their actions.

- Unbelieving and fearful Gentiles
- Trying to save the ship
- Waking Jonah roughly
- Casting lots
- Putting Jonah on trial
- Continuing to row against the storm
- Washing their hands of Jonah
- Throwing him overboard
- Bearing witness to Jonah's God

NINEVEH/NINEVITES

We have already fleshed out Nineveh in detail in Part 1, so we'll just boil down what we know into simple elements:

- A Gentile nation
- A wicked and violent people
- Enemies of Israel

Their actions include:
- Fasting
- Mourning and repenting

KING OF NINEVEH

The king's actions include:

- Being tested for 40 days
- Being tested to see if he will submit to God and obey
- Fasting
- Mourning and repenting
- Calling his people to repent

If the *sar puhi* ritual was being carried out, then:

- He was the substitute chosen to take God's wrath
- He is king, and yet not king
- The kingdom is in his hands, yet it isn't his to claim
- He understood that he must die to save his nation

THREE DAYS

We will treat the three-days picture as a separate element from the third day element. A span of time defined by three days crops up a number of times in the Old Testament; and if we boil down the context of those verses, we can see that a three-day period signifies:

- A measure of space or time needed for separation or sanctification.
    - Laban took his flocks three days' journey from Jacob's flock so that there would be no interbreeding. (Genesis 30:36)
    - Jacob was given a three-day head-start when he fled from Laban, his father-in-law. (Genesis 31:22)
    - "...Please, let us go three days' journey into the wilderness, that we may sacrifice to the Lord our God." (Exodus 3:18, 5:3, 8:27)
    - The children of Israel were to be sanctified for two days to prepare them to meet the Lord on the third day on Mount Sinai. Men had to keep themselves from women in order to be considered sanctified. (Exodus 19:10-11, 15; cf 1 Samuel 21:5)
- A measure of time needed for testing faithfulness or obedience
    - Abraham and Isaac journeyed three days to Mount Moriah (Genesis 22:4). It is a time of testing of Abraham's obedience and faithfulness, whether he will trust God and offer up his son.
    - There are a number of three-day intervals on the Exodus journey, involving a time of testing the people's faithfulness and perserverance. Three days into the wilderness, the children of Israel encounter their first test of faithfulness and reliance on God at Marah. (Exodus 15:22-26) As they set out from Mount Sinai, the ark goes ahead of them three days to search out a resting place. During that three-day interval trek to the next camp, the people begin complaining and suffer judgment at Taberah (Numbers 10:33, 11:1-3)

When we see what a three-day span of time signifies, then it seems appropriate that Jonah should have spent three days in the belly of the fish to accomplish these purposes. It also adds a dimension of understanding to what three days in the grave accomplished in Christ's ministry.

The three-day interval culminates in the third day, but the third day itself has specific characteristics and actions attached to it. Let's look at the third day by itself in Scripture.

THE THIRD DAY

From the following verses, we can draw three main conclusions as to what the third day signified in the Old Testament:

- The day of Creation when the land is drawn out of the seas
    - » Figurative of Israel (the Land) being drawn out of the Gentile nations (the Seas)
    - » Marks the beginning of new life (literally, plants begin to grow)
- A day of verdict and decision that brings about a turning point or a change of life direction
    - » Abraham prepares to sacrifice Isaac on the third day of the journey when they get to Mount Moriah (Genesis 22:4). This ends with a reprieve as a ram is provided in Isaac's place; Isaac is restored to his father; and Abraham's act is counted as an act of faith.
    - » On the third day, Simeon and Levi render judgment on Shechem for the rape of their sister, Dinah (Genesis 34:25). The vindication of Dinah also leads to Simeon and Levi's loss of blessing.
    - » On the third day, the verdict is pronounced upon Pharoah's baker and butler according to the prophecy of Joseph (Genesis 40:20). This leads to the restoration of the butler and the death of the baker.
    - » Joseph holds his brothers captive for three days in judgment, and on the third day announces his decision concerning them (Genesis 42:17-18). This is the beginning of the confrontation that leads to Joseph revealing his identity to his brothers and the salvation and revival of Israel, a major turning point in history.
    - » The waters of separation must be applied specifically on the third day in cleansing a person who is defiled by touching the dead, if the person is to be purified (Numbers 19:12, 19; 31:19). Without this third-day cleansing, the person must remain separated from a relationship with God and the congregation.
    - » On the third day, the people with whom Joshua makes a covenant of peace are found to be Canaanites (Joshua 9:15-16). This is a turning point in Israel's history, because they do not turn the Canaanites out of the land but make them slaves instead.
    - » Esther and the Jews fast and pray for three days; and on the third

day, Esther presents herself before the king. As a result, the Jewish people are saved from Haman's plot (Esther 4:16).

- A day of repentance, reconciliation, and restoration which marks a turning point in someone's life.
  - » Hezekiah is granted healing, an extended life, and deliverance from the Assyrians, and is restored to the presence of the Lord on the third day (2 Kings 20).
  - » *"Come, and let us return to the LORD; for He has torn, but He will heal us; He has stricken, but He will bind us up. After two days He will revive us; on the third day He will raise us up, that we may live in His sight."* (Hosea 6:1-2)
- Resurrection (While Hosea 6:1-2 certainly implies resurrection, the verses are not necessarily considered proof texts for resurrection in Pharisaical doctrine. We add this concept of resurrection to the third-day context because of what we know of the end picture of Christ as it connects with the sign of Jonah.)

Now add these contexts to Jonah's experience. In response to Jonah's repentance and turning, God decides to restore him to land. On the third day, Jonah is drawn out of the sea (spit out, really) and given a new beginning which will ultimately bring a turning point in the lives of the Ninevites as well.

Before we leave the third-day element, I want to note that this element appears in one other very subtle way in the Jonah text. Do you remember how Jonah identifies himself to the sailors? He says, *"I am a Hebrew; and I fear the LORD, the God of heaven, who made the sea and the dry land."* (Jonah 1:9) On what day did the God of heaven make the sea and dry land? On the third day. What follows in the narrative is the passage-through-water element which we will study next. The passage through water is initiated by this reference to the third day at the beginning of the sequence, and is completed with Jonah being spit out onto land on the third day (Jonah 2:10). So the third-day element really encapsulates the passage-through-water element.

A PASSAGE THROUGH WATER

This is a very complex element, and it is a core picture, not just in the life of Christ but in Christian doctrine. Out of this Old Testament picture, we get the New Testament practice of immersion baptism.

It vexes me when I hear pastors and Bible teachers say that baptism is purely a New Testament sacrament that John the Baptist began of his own volition. The Pharisees' question in John 1:25 shows that they recognized what John the Baptist was doing, it was not an unknown thing, and that it was an act by which the Messiah would be known when He came. So where did their understanding of this come from in the Old Testament?

As I build the elemental understanding of a passage through water, I want you to recognize that this is the picture of baptism that the Pharisees were seeing. This is John's baptism—the Old Covenant version that is forerunner to the immersion baptism practiced as part of the New Covenant.

The basic picture unfolds in Jonah 1.

- A public confession and identification with God
- A act of judgment (Jonah on trial before the sailors)
- A man going into the water, likened to death
- A man being saved when he enters the vessel of rescue (the fish)
- A man entering or re-dedicating himself to a covenant (keeping vows)
- A man being drawn out of the water, restored to life on land, likened to resurrection

Now let's add the context of other pictures of passages through water to that. These include the third day of Creation, Flood account, and the Red Sea crossing. We will look at each of these in turn and then gather all the contexts together with Jonah to create one picture.

The Third Day of Creation

We have already mentioned some of this in the element of the third day:

- God gathers together a *mikveh* of waters which He calls the Seas. *Mikveh* is the Hebrew word for the gathering of waters. It describes something that has been separated and gathered together for a singular purpose.
- Out of the *mikveh* of waters God draws the land.
- The breaking of *mikveh* waters allows the emergence of new land and new life. There is an act of transformation being accomplished.

Mikveh is a sub-element that begins here in Genesis and builds out of the passage-through-water imagery, so I will discuss it as a separate element after I get through the main pictures.

The Flood Account

- Associated with an act of divine judgment
- People under judgment going into the waters (to death)
  - » Separation of the righteous from the unrighteous
- A few being saved in a vessel of rescue—an ark
  - » Salvation of the righteous
  - » A gathering together of the righteous as a distinct body of believers
- Those found righteous being drawn out of the water
  - » Restored to the land
  - » Given a renewal of life
- A covenant is established—the Noahic covenant
- There is a third-day parallel in Genesis 8, where the waters are receding so that land appears. In that passage, we also see:
  - » A ship afloat on a windy sea
  - » The dove—a messenger sent over the waters to seek new life

Peter speaks of Noah and the ark as a type of baptism, speaking of how *"the Divine longsuffering waited in the days of Noah, while the ark was being prepared, in which a few, that is, eight souls, were saved through water. There is also an antitype which now saves us—baptism (not the removal of the filth of the flesh, but the answer of a good conscience toward God), through the resurrection of Jesus Christ"* (1 Peter 3:20-21). The picture of resurrection is connected to the act of being drawn out of the water.

The Red Sea Crossing

The Red Sea is a highly significant passage through water. We also know from the New Testament that the Red Sea crossing of the Exodus is a type of baptism.

> *"Moreover, brethren, I do not want you to be unaware that all our fathers were under the cloud, all passed through the sea, all were baptized into Moses in the cloud and in the sea, all ate the same spiritual food, and all drank the same spiritual drink..."—1 Corinthians 10:1-4*

In the Exodus account, we see the repeated imagery:

- Judgment between the evil and righteous
- Salvation and separation of the righteous
- Gathering together of a people into a new body of believers

- Beginning of new life
- Entrance into a covenant relationship—the Mosaic Covenant

The Jewish people took all this imagery associated with passages through water and translated it into a physical practice called *tevilah mikveh*, or simply *mikveh* for short, and it is still practiced today. *Tevilah mikveh* means bodily immersion in a gathering of waters, and the understanding of this practice adds to the picture of the passage through water. Let's expand the picture to include the *mikveh* elements.

MIKVEH

The practice of *mikveh* has two aspects. Out of the Law comes the physical practice of immersion baptism (what the religious leaders recognized in John's baptism). Out of the prophetic books, it becomes an expression of hope for a Messiah.

Mikveh as Baptism

Tevilah mikveh is used for the purpose of sanctification and spiritual cleansing, or in conjunction with repenting and putting away the sin of the old year in preparation for the Day of Atonement. As Peter says, it is performed not for the removal of the filth of the flesh, but the answer of a good conscience toward God.

A *mikveh* is also performed on the occasion of entering into covenants such as conversion to Judaism and marriage. In such cases, the act of *mikveh* marked an irrevocable change in covenant status and a new beginning.

The only requirement for the *mikveh* bath is that it must be a gathering of living water (running water) tied to a renewable source such as a spring or fountain that can carry the uncleanness away without defiling the bath, as prescribed in the Law:

> "Nevertheless a spring or a cistern, in which there is plenty [mikveh] of water, shall be clean..."—Leviticus 11:36

Because the water continually renews, unclean things can be put into the *mikveh* bath without making it unclean. Therefore, it is able to offer continual cleansing.

Mikveh as Hope

Apart from the Law, this word, *mikveh*, is translated as hope. At the inauguration of Solomon as king, David uses the word, *mikveh,* in a highly figurative way.

> *"For we are aliens and pilgrims before You, as were all our fathers; our days on earth are as a shadow, and without hope [mikveh]."*
> —*1 Chronicles 29:17*

Here *mikveh* is translated as the word "hope" (the KJV translates it as "none abiding"). *Mikveh* becomes a metaphorical concept rather than a tangible thing like seas or baths of water.

In a beautiful turning of words, David raises before the Lord the issue of Israel being without *mikveh*—without gathering as a nation. He calls the children of Israel aliens and pilgrims, as shifting as a gathering of shadows.

To be without *mikveh* is to be without hope. If you are not gathered into one body or nation, then you are without permanent status, like an alien having no rights in the land. Being gathered together as a people of God is a vital function of *mikveh* baptism. It is our means of declaring our identification with fellow believers. It gives us a sense of permanence in the family of God and rights to claim the blessings and responsibilities for our part of the covenant relationship.

This verse is also an expression of being immersed in the hope for the coming King. David's prayer projects a prophetic vision of a future King who would be *Mikveh Israel*, the Hope and Gatherer of the nation.

Jeremiah also speaks of a savior figure as the Hope of Israel:

> *"O the Hope [mikveh] of Israel, his Savior in time of trouble, why should You be like a stranger in the land, and like a traveler who turns aside to tarry for a night?"—Jeremiah 14:8*

> *"O LORD, the hope [mikveh] of Israel, all who forsake You shall be ashamed. 'Those who depart from Me shall be written in the earth, because they have forsaken the LORD, the fountain of living waters.'"*
> —*Jeremiah 17:13*

David's prophetic vision of a coming King who will gather the people into an enduring body and lasting kingdom gives us the connection of Messianic hope to baptism. Jeremiah identifies *Mikveh Israel* as God Himself. Is *Mikveh Israel* the Messianic King, God, or both? He is the embodiment of both.

While we, in this age, have not yet come into the kingdom, we are the gathering of those drawn out of the waters and cleansed by the living waters. We are not drawn out of just a bath of water, but out of *Mikveh*

Israel, the Hope of Israel, Jesus Christ, Who is the embodiment of our identity, our cleansing, and our hope in the day of judgment. In Him lies our vision and hope of a coming kingdom in which there will be peace, permanence, and stability, and where we will have rights as children and heirs of the kingdom. He is our *mikveh*, our hope.

Summary of the Passage through Water/Mikveh

If we put the bullets points for all three passages through water together with the associated element of *mikveh*, we get the following list:

- Act of baptism
    - Beginning with public confession and identification with God
    - Going into the water under judgment
        - Gathering of waters (*mikveh*) called Seas
        - Symbolic of the separation of Israel from the nations (believer from unbelievers)
        - Likened to death
    - Salvation of the righteous by a vessel of rescue (ark, fish)
    - Being drawn out of the water
        - Restored to land
        - Marks a new beginning/renewal of life
        - Likened to resurrection
- A symbolic act representing the response of a good conscience toward God
    - For identification with a body of believers
    - For entering into or renewing a covenant relationship
    - For sanctification and separation
    - For cleansing and ritual purification
    - Facilitated by a bath drawn from a source of living water
- Associated with a third-day theme in Genesis 8
    - A ship afloat on a windy sea
    - The dove—a messenger sent over the waters
- Associated with the hope for a Messianic King to gather the people into a lasting, eternal kingdom

Seeing this picture in all its associated elements, I cannot understand why Christian leaders and teachers still maintain that baptism is a wholly New Testament sacrament and "new thing" in Jesus' day. It is actually a very old understanding that was carried forward into a New Testament context. Just as Christ's death did away with the need for continual sacrifices, so His death did away with the need for continual immersions. In Him, we are baptized once and for all.

THE BOOTH

In Jonah 4:5, Jonah makes himself a rough shelter or booth, which is the Hebrew word, *sukkah*. The imagery of the *sukkah* builds out of the Old Testament beginning in Genesis.

> *"And Jacob journeyed to Succoth, built himself a house, and made booths [sukkot] for his livestock. Therefore the name of the place is called Succoth."—Genesis 33:17*

The core picture is Jacob in his centrally-located big tent, surrounded by his flocks housed in small booths all around him. So extensive are his stockyards that the place is simply called Succoth, "the booths."

This core picture then translates to God and His flock during the Exodus, with God in His Tabernacle and His people camped around Him in their booths. When He gives them the Law during this journey, there is included a command to preserve this picture for future generations with the Feast of Tabernacles, called in Hebrew, Sukkot (pronounced sue-coat), the booths.

> *"Speak to the children of Israel, saying: 'The fifteenth day of this seventh month shall be the Feast of Tabernacles [Sukkot] for seven days to the LORD. . . . You shall dwell in booths for seven days. All who are native Israelites shall dwell in booths, that your generations may know that I made the children of Israel dwell in booths when I brought them out of the land of Egypt: I am the LORD your God.'"—Leviticus 23:34, 42-43*

When the children of Israel keep the Feast of Tabernacles in the Land of Israel, the booths are no longer just rough shelters. They are decorated with branches, vines, and harvested fruits. The people spend a week rejoicing in their booths in acknowledgement of the Lord's provision and protection from year to year.

This picture of the Feast of Tabernacles reaches its greatest expression in 2 Chronicles 5-7. Solomon times the dedication of the Temple to coincide with the feast, at which time the Shekinah glory comes down to fill the Temple. So the picture associated with that feast becomes one of God in His glory in the Temple, the Davidic King reigning on the throne, and Israel gathered about, rejoicing in their booths. It is a prophetic picture of a kingdom yet to come that was meant to be preserved throughout Israel's generations until it is fulfilled by the Messiah at His second coming.

Here in Jonah 4, we see Jonah rejoicing in his plant-shaded booth. That picture invokes the imagery of the Feast of Tabernacles and the glorious illustration of a kingdom to come. God creates this picture by preparing the leafy plant to grow up over the booth.

Summary of the booth

- Literally, a rough lean-to or shelter, also called a booth.
- A man rejoicing beneath a branch-covered booth is a prophetic picture of the Messiah's kingdom. The totality of the picture includes God in His Temple, the Davidic King on His throne, and all Israel camped about them.

THE PLANT

The plant here is the *kikayon*, akin to a castor-plant or a gourd. It is a beautiful, leafy plant with tender, succulent stalks that, if damaged, will cause the plant to die.

The suggested Hebrew root word for *kikayon* is *kayah*, which means nauseous, perhaps from the reaction to ingesting the plant. This creates an interesting picture of a plant representing God's provision and protection, while at the same time producing a nauseous fruit. The lesson God makes out of this plant certainly leaves Jonah with a bad taste in his mouth.

Figuratively, a plant can represent a nation that springs up quickly and overruns other nations, glorifies itself, and is cut down by another agent (hence, the worm). Rebellious Israel is portrayed as just such a plant.

Summary of the plant

It is symbolic of:

- A hard lesson in God's provision and protection
- A nation that springs up quickly and overruns other nations
- A nation that glorifies itself and is cut down by another nation
- A figurative expression of rebellious Israel
- The plant-shaded booth invokes the imagery of the Feast of Tabernacles and a picture of the Messianic kingdom.

THE WORM

Having prepared the plant, God then prepares the worm to eat away at the plant so that it withers and dies.

Worms, in general, are agents of decay and destruction associated with death, the grave, and corruption of a body. In this case, the worm eats away at the plant so that it dies, and in doing so, also corrupts the picture of the kingdom the plant represents.

Worms can be worms, or worms can be men. Men who are lowly or despised are considered worm-like in their character or condition.

> *"If I wait for the grave as my house, if I make my bed in the darkness, if I say to corruption, 'You are my father,' And to the worm, 'You are my mother and my sister,' Where then is my hope? As for my hope, who can see it?"—Job 17:13-15*

> *"How much less man, who is a maggot, and a son of man, who is a worm?"—Job 25:6*

> *"But I am a worm, and no man; a reproach of men, and despised by the people."—Psalm 22:6*

> *"'Fear not, you worm Jacob, you men of Israel! I will help you,' says the LORD and your Redeemer, the Holy One of Israel."—Isaiah 41:14*

The particular worm mentioned in Jonah is the *towla*, the scarlet worm, from which the scarlet dye is extracted for coloring the Tabernacle fabrics. There is a picture of Christ in this worm that I will explain in the next chapter.

Summary of the worm

- The agent that eats away at the plant so that it dies
- The human agent who corrupts or destroys, who may be divinely appointed for that task
- A human who is lowly, despised, or rejected

There are a number interpretive layers to the booth–plant–worm–wind scenario that God creates in Jonah 4. I discuss these in the next chapter when we put these building blocks together.

The Reconstruction Process

We have now deconstructed the narrative into basic who-what-when-where-action elements. We have studied each of those in depth and drawn a small picture of the greater context they represent. Now we are going to use these elements like building blocks to create the pictures of Christ out of the narrative of Jonah.

Keep in mind the following guidelines:

1) Different pictures of Christ's life will be made out of different combinations of blocks. We may use blocks 1, 3, 5, 6, and 7 for one picture, and blocks 5, 6, 7, 11, and 12 for another.

2) One passage may contain multiple pictures of Christ, depending on which elements in that passage we choose to combine. We may use some, but not all the elements in any given passage.

3) The sequence of the build must follow the sequence of the narrative, although some verses in the narrative may be skipped over.

4) In regards to the people, the building block may include just an aspect of their basic character or one of their actions. Each action must be treated as a separate building block. One picture of Christ might include the picture of the man (Jonah) sleeping in a ship, but will not include the same man prophesying to Gentiles.

For review, here is the list of the specific building blocks we will be using in various combinations:

- God
- Jonah
- Dove
- Ship
- Sea
- East Wind
- The Great Fish
- Sailors
- Ninevites
- King of Nineveh
- Passage through Water
- Three Days
- Third Day
- Booth
- Plant
- Worm

So that you will appreciate the task the Jewish people had in trying to extract the pictures of Christ out of Old Testament narratives like Jonah, look at the full list of narrative elements on the following pages. See how many you can associate with the Gospel accounts of Jesus' life. Then go to the next chapter.

God		Commanding a prophet to go to a wicked people
		Hurling down a storm
		Calming the storm
		Preparing a fish as a vessel of rescue
		Telling the fish to return Jonah to land
		Relenting in judgment
		Confronting Jonah
		Preparing a plant
		Preparing a worm
		Preparing an east wind
Jonah		A Hebrew man from the northern Kingdom of Israel
		A prophet
		A *tsiyr* (terrifying messenger meant to bring health)
		Associated with a passage through water (baptism)
		His coming is a sign
	Dove	His name means "dove"
		A messenger sent over the waters that brings back good news of new life
		A sacrifice
		One mourning in his own iniquity
		One who flaps about foolishly
		One who finds no resting place
		One exiled to Assyria
		One who returns to God
		Symbolic of disobedient Israel
	Actions	Fleeing from God
		Sleeping through a storm
		Being put on trial
		Offering himself as a sacrifice to save others
		Thrown over in judgment
		Going down into the sea
		Spending three days in the belly of the fish
		Repenting
		Being restored to land on the third day
		Walking out of the wilderness
		Prophesying in Nineveh
		Calling the people to be *haphak*-ed
		Getting angrier and angrier
		Building a booth
		Rejoicing under a plant-shaded booth
		Being left with a rebuke

Sailors	Actions	Unbelieving, fearful Gentiles Trying to save the ship Waking Jonah roughly from sleep Casting lots Putting Jonah on trial Continuing to row against the storm Washing their hands of Jonah Throwing him over Bearing witness of Jonah's God
Ship		A literal ship Carrier of merchandise and luxury goods A source of perceived strength Broken by the east wind Saved by God in a time of storm A place of refuge threatened in a hostile environment
Sea		A literal sea Figurative of Gentile nations
Great Fish		Literal fish Vessel of rescue
Nineveh/ Ninevites		A Gentile nation People fasting, mourning, and repenting
King of Nineveh	Actions	A king The substitute chosen to take God's wrath Tested for 40 days to see if he will submit to God and obey Fasting Mourning & repenting Calling his people to repent
Three Days		Space or time needed for separation/sanctification A measure of time needed for testing faithfulness or obedience
Third Day		Earth being drawn out of the Sea Figurative of Israel being drawn out of the Gentile nations Marks the beginning of new life A day of verdict and decision that brings a turning point A day of repentance, reconciliation, and restoration

Passage through Water	Mikveh/Baptism	Public confession and identification with God Facilitated by gathering of waters (*mikveh*, seas) Going into the water likened to death The righteous saved if found in a vessel of rescue Being drawn out of the water likened to resurrection Beginning/renewal of life A symbolic act representing the response of a good conscience toward God For identification with a body of believers For entering into or renewing a covenant relationship For sanctification and separation For cleansing and ritual purification Facilitated by a bath drawn from a source of living water Expression of hope
Booth		Rough shelter or booth; expands to a man rejoicing under a shady booth as a picture of the kingdom
Plant		A hard lesson in God's provision and protection A nation that springs up quickly, overruns other nations, glorifies itself, and is cut down by another agent Symbolic of rebellious Israel
Worm		The agent that eats away at the plant so that it dies A divinely appointed agent who corrupts or destroys A human who is lowly, despised, or rejected
East Wind		An agent of judgment and punishment Created by God, and can only be calmed by God

Pictures of Christ in Jonah

Scenario 1: A Prophet with a Ministry of Baptism

> "Now the word of the LORD came to Jonah the son of Amittai, saying, 'Rise, go to Nineveh, that great city, and cry out against it; for their wickedness has come up before Me.' . . . And Jonah began to enter the city on the first day's walk. Then he cried out and said, 'Yet forty days, and Nineveh shall be overthrown!' So the people of Nineveh believed God, proclaimed a fast, and put on sackcloth, from the greatest to the least of them."—Jonah 1:1-2; 3:4-5

Boiling the narrative down: The man is a prophet of God, a messenger sent to deliver a hard message to a wicked people. The man's name means the dove, and his arrival is a sign. He crosses the river and upon reaching the bank on the east side, begins prophesying as he enters the city. He warns them that God's impending judgment is upon them and that they will be *haphak*-ed. The people respond by confessing their sins and repenting.

Note: I skipped the sequence in Chapters 1–2 involving the ship, storm, sailors, and fish, which would not have happened if the prophet had been obedient. Chapter 3 picks up again as if none of that ever happened.

Building blocks: Jonah, Ninevites

New Testament Parallel

> "In those days John the Baptist came preaching in the wilderness of Judea, and saying, 'Repent, for the kingdom of heaven is at hand!' . . . Then Jerusalem, all Judea, and all the region around the Jordan went out to him and were baptized by him in the Jordan, confessing their sins. . . ."
> —Matthew 3:1-2, 5-6

> "Now this is the testimony of John, when the Jews sent priests and Levites from Jerusalem to ask him, 'Who are you?' He confessed, and did not deny, but confessed, 'I am not the Christ.' And they asked him, 'What then? Are you Elijah?' He said, 'I am not.' 'Are you the Prophet?' And he answered, 'No.' . . . And they asked him, saying, 'Why then do you baptize if you are not the Christ, nor Elijah, nor the Prophet?'"—John 1:19-25

"I did not know Him; but that He should be revealed to Israel, therefore I came baptizing with water."—John 1:31

Jonah and John the Baptist

Jonah strongly identifies with John the Baptist in the role of the prophet sent with a hard message to an unrepentant people. Both come out of the wilderness, both cross over to the east side of a river (in John's case it is the east side of the Jordan River at Bethabara), and both prophesy there. Many of Israel, like the Ninevites, respond wholeheartedly to the prophet by confessing their sins. Thus, Israel becomes something of a counterpart to the Ninevites in the scenario. Those who are unrepentant will be rebuked by the example of the Ninevites who repented, as it says:

> *"The men of Nineveh will rise up in the judgment with this generation and condemn it, because they repented at the preaching of Jonah; and indeed a greater than Jonah is here."—Matthew 12:41 (cf Luke 11:32)*

The Sign of Jonah

Jonah the prophet is associated with a picture of baptism while John the prophet has a ministry of baptism, and that baptism is meant to be a sign. When we think of the sign of Jonah, we think about the three days and three nights in the belly of the fish, but that sequence is really the *mikveh*/baptism sequence as a whole. The specificity of three days and three nights points to a particular fulfillment, but the act of baptism overall is a sign, as John explains:

> *"I did not know Him; but that He should be revealed to Israel, therefore I came baptizing with water."—John 1:31.*

Baptism is a means of identification. That understanding is part of that small picture we pulled from the Old Testament contexts. It is a means of identifying with God's people overall, but also identifying with the hope of a coming One Who would be the gatherer of Israel—the Messiah.

Therefore, the *mikveh*/baptism itself is the sign of Jonah, or should I say, the sign of the *yownah* (dove).

The Baptism Sequence of Jonah 1–2

We skipped much of Jonah 1 and 2 when talking about John the Baptist for a reason. While Jonah is the one making the passage through water, John the Baptist is not the one being baptized; Jesus is. Jonah and John the Baptist only share the association with a passage through water/baptism ministry. In Chapters 1–2, Jonah shifts from being the persona of John the Baptist to the persona of Christ.

Scenario 2: Christ's Baptism

Christ goes through two baptisms in His ministry: a literal, physical one at the start of His ministry and a figurative, spiritual one at His death. When Jesus speaks of His death to His disciples, He speaks of it as a baptism (Matthew 20:22-23). When speaking to the Pharisees about His death, He tells them that the only sign they would receive was the sign of Jonah (Luke 11:29; Matthew 12:39).

Even while Jonah represents John the Baptist in Chapters 1-3, as I just showed you, now he represents Christ for the section we skipped in Chapters 1-2, in the sequence involving the ship, storm, sailors, and fish. The prophetic pictures of both baptisms are found in this same passage, depending on which building blocks from that passage we combine. The literal baptism is the lesser of the two pictures, which is what I will show here.

> *"So he said to them, 'I am a Hebrew; and I fear the LORD, the God of heaven, who made the sea and the dry land.'.... So they picked up Jonah and threw him into the sea, and the sea ceased from its raging.... Now the LORD had prepared a great fish to swallow Jonah.... And he said: 'I cried out to the LORD because of my affliction, and He answered me. Out of the belly of Sheol I cried, and You heard my voice.... I went down to the moorings of the mountains; the earth with its bars closed behind me forever; Yet You have brought up my life from the pit, O LORD, my God.... But I will sacrifice to You with the voice of thanksgiving; I will pay what I have vowed. Salvation is of the LORD.' So the LORD spoke to the fish, and it vomited Jonah onto dry land."—Jonah 1:9, 15, 17 ; 2:2, 6, 9-10*

Boiling down the narrative: This is the basic baptism sequence. It begins with a public confession of faith and identification with God the Creator. Then the person goes into the water, as under judgment, likened to death, and associated with an act of repentance. He is saved when he is taken into the vessel of rescue (fish). It is through the work of that vessel of rescue that he is restored to life in the land, likened to resurrection. This baptism sequence marks the start of Jonah's ministry to Nineveh.

Jonah, the dove, is associated with this practice of *mikveh*/baptism in the minds of Jewish people.

Remember, *mikveh* was performed for the following reasons:
   » For sanctification and separation
   » For cleansing and ritual purification

» Identification with God's people

» When entering new covenants or rededicating oneself to a covenant with God, as many Jewish people do at Yom Kippur (Day of Atonement), performing a physical act of *mikveh* as a sign of their spiritual repentance after the model of Jonah

Building Blocks: Jonah, Passage through Water, Dove

New Testament Parallel:

"I [John the Baptist] did not know Him; but that He should be revealed to Israel, therefore I came baptizing with water. And John bore witness, saying, 'I saw the Spirit descending from heaven like a dove, and He remained upon Him. I did not know Him, but He who sent me to baptize with water said to me, "Upon whom you see the Spirit descending, and remaining on Him, this is He who baptizes with the Holy Spirit."'"—John 1:31-33

"Then Jesus came from Galilee to John at the Jordan to be baptized by him. . . . When He had been baptized, Jesus came up immediately from the water; and behold, the heavens were opened to Him, and He saw the Spirit of God descending like a dove and alighting upon Him. And suddenly a voice came from heaven, saying, 'This is My beloved Son, in whom I am well pleased.'"—Matthew 3:13, 16-17

Jesus' *mikveh* is an appropriate mark to the start of His ministry, for sanctification and separation to that task. It is also necessary for identification—His identification with the people, and the people's identification of Him. The physical arrival of a *yownah* (dove) sets Jesus' baptism apart from the rest and verifies Who He is. This is why I broke the dove out as a separate element from Jonah in the building blocks. Jonah parallels Christ in this scene, but not the Spirit, Who is embodied in the dove. Christ and the Spirit are two and yet one, as members of the Trinity, even as Jonah and the dove are two and yet one.

It is interesting to think of the dove in this scenario as a messenger. Like the dove in Genesis 8 who brings Noah the olive leaf, olive being the oil with which kings and priests are anointed, this dove signals the appearance of the Anointed One. The dove is also a *tsiyr* in that its arrival signals the beginning of trials for the One on which it landed, but the end of those trials would bring healing and health for all God's people.

Scenario 3: Christ's Temptations

The scene in Nineveh immediately follows the baptism sequence in Jonah. Even so, Christ's baptism is followed immediately by His Temptations. In this scenario, the King of Nineveh becomes the parallel to Christ.

> *"And Jonah began to enter the city on the first day's walk. Then he cried out and said, 'Yet forty days, and Nineveh shall be overthrown!' . . . Then word came to the king of Nineveh; and he arose from his throne and laid aside his robe, covered himself with sackcloth and sat in ashes. And he caused it to be proclaimed and published throughout Nineveh by the decree of the king and his nobles, saying, Let neither man nor beast, herd nor flock, taste anything; do not let them eat, or drink water. But let man and beast be covered with sackcloth, and cry mightily to God; yes, let every one turn from his evil way and from the violence that is in his hands. Who can tell if God will turn and relent, and turn away from His fierce anger, so that we may not perish?"—Jonah 3:4, 6-9*

Boiling down the narrative: The king is the most prominent figure in this passage. The prophet arrives with the pronouncement of impending doom, and a 40-day trial begins to see if the king will be "overthrown." The king commits himself to extreme fasting and commands the people to repent from their evil ways. Unless the king and his people submit to the will of God and repent, they will perish.

If we add the context of the *sar puhi* ritual to the picture, then the king is a substitute. He is king, and yet not king. The kingdom is at his command, yet not his to claim. He is the one chosen to take the brunt of God's wrath and thus spare the nation. Though this is extra-biblical in nature, it dovetails perfectly with the picture of Christ that God is building in this scenario.

Building Blocks: King of Nineveh

New Testament Parallel:

> *"Then Jesus was led up by the Spirit into the wilderness to be tempted by the devil. And when He had fasted forty days and forty nights, afterward He was hungry. Now when the tempter came to Him, he said, 'If You are the Son of God, command that these stones become bread.' But He answered and said, 'It is written, "Man shall not live by bread alone, but by every word that proceeds from the mouth of God."' Then the devil took Him up into the holy city, set Him on the pinnacle of the temple, and said to Him, 'If You are the Son of God, throw Yourself down.' . . . Jesus said to*

> him, 'It is written again, "You shall not tempt the LORD your God."' Again, the devil took Him up on an exceedingly high mountain, and showed Him all the kingdoms of the world and their glory. And he said to Him, 'All these things I will give You if You will fall down and worship me.' Then Jesus said to him, 'Away with you, Satan! For it is written, "You shall worship the LORD your God, and Him only you shall serve."' Then the devil left Him, and behold, angels came and ministered to Him. . . . From that time Jesus began to preach and to say, 'Repent, for the kingdom of heaven is at hand.'"—Matthew 4:1-11, 17

It seems appropriate that Christ as King identifies with the King of Nineveh in this scenario, even if the King of Nineveh is a heathen Gentile. God sometimes uses Gentile kings to create pictures of Christ in the Old Testament.

Both undergo 40 days of trial and fasting. Both are being tested to see if they understand Who God is and if they will submit to His will. If they fail in obedience, the kings with their kingdoms will be overthrown.

Both are kings and yet not kings. Their respective kingdoms are theirs to command, and yet taking those kingdoms is not what they seek in this trial. Both understand that the kingdom is not theirs to claim. The only focus they have is on submission to God and calling the people to repent.

Scenario 4: A Man Asleep in a Boat in a Storm

"But the LORD sent out a great wind on the sea, and there was a mighty tempest on the sea, so that the ship was about to be broken up. Then the mariners were afraid; and every man cried out to his god, and threw the cargo that was in the ship into the sea, to lighten the load. But Jonah had gone down into the lowest parts of the ship, had lain down, and was fast asleep. So the captain came to him, and said to him, 'What do you mean, sleeper? Arise, call on your God; perhaps your God will consider us, so that we may not perish.' . . . And he said to them, 'Pick me up and throw me into the sea; then the sea will become calm for you. For I know that this great tempest is because of me.' . . . So they picked up Jonah and threw him into the sea, and the sea ceased from its raging. Then the men feared the LORD exceedingly, and offered a sacrifice to the LORD and took vows."
—*Jonah 1:4-6, 12, 15-16*

Boiling the narrative down: A group of men are caught in a ship as a great storm arises. The ship is ready to sink. One man is sleeping in the hold, oblivious to the crisis. The fearful crew wakes him roughly, imploring him to do what he can to calm the storm. He provides a solution that calms the storm. As a result, they fear his God exceedingly.

Building blocks: God, Jonah, Ship, Storm, Sea, Sailors

New Testament Parallel:

"Now when they had left the multitude, they took Him along in the boat as He was. And other little boats were also with Him. And a great windstorm arose, and the waves beat into the boat, so that it was already filling. But He was in the stern, asleep on a pillow. And they awoke Him and said to Him, 'Teacher, do You not care that we are perishing?' Then He arose and rebuked the wind, and said to the sea, 'Peace, be still!' And the wind ceased and there was a great calm. But He said to them, 'Why are you so fearful? How is it that you have no faith?' And they feared exceedingly, and said to one another, 'Who can this be, that even the wind and the sea obey Him!'"—*Mark 4:36-41*

The difficulty in seeing this picture of Christ is that Jonah plays his part, and God calms the sea. In the New Testament parallel, Christ plays *both* parts—Jonah *and* God. He is the figure of Jonah asleep in the boat, and also God calming the sea. Unless you understand that Christ is equally man and God, you would not put this picture together from the Jonah text.

Scenario 5: Christ's Death and Resurrection

The picture begins in Jonah 1:4 with the baptism sequence and stretches all the way to Jonah 3:2. It connects with more of the details, and engages many more of the building blocks than the previous picture of Jesus' literal baptism. Rather than copying the entirety of those Bible passages, I will just summarize the picture.

Boiling down the narrative: We begin with a ship afloat in the sea. A great storm blows up, and the sailors are afraid the ship will go down. One man is identified as the cause of the storm. He stands on trial before the heathen Gentile sailors who ask him to identify himself and are horrified when they find out who he is.

A discussion ensues over what to do stop the storm. The man tells them to throw him into the sea, because he must die to turn back God's wrath and calm the storm. They understand that the storm is an issue between this man and his God, and has nothing to do with them, so they are reluctant to throw him overboard. For this reason, the Gentile sailors decide to keep rowing against the storm, until they find they cannot prevail against it. Then they decide to wash their hands of him, pray for God's mercy on themselves for condemning an innocent man to death, and then throw him over. Because Jonah's prophetic words come true (the sea becomes calm after they throw him over), the sailors acknowledge his God and carry the story to many nations.

The man then spends three days and three nights in the sea, preserved in the belly of the great fish. His prayers are the words of the Davidic king, who sees himself as going down into death, yet not to the corruption of death, and being raised up out of the pit. Before God, the man agrees to complete the mission which he vowed to do, and God has the fish restore him to life in the land of the living on the third day. The man then goes to a Gentile nation, facilitating its repentance and turning to God.

Building Blocks: Sea, Storm, Ship, Sailors, Jonah, Passage through Water, Three Days, Third Day, Ninevites

New Testament Parallel

Israel is a nation afloat in the "sea" of the Roman Empire. A storm rises that is threatening their ship, which the leaders are afraid will be broken up and lost in that Gentile sea. One man, Jesus, is identified as the cause of the storm, which reaches a peak when He resurrects a man from the dead. Jesus is questioned as to Who He is, and when He tells them, they are horrified.

A discussion ensues over what to do with Him.

> *"Then the chief priests and the Pharisees gathered a council and said, 'What shall we do? For this Man works many signs. If we let Him alone like this, everyone will believe in Him, and the Romans will come and take away both our place and nation.'"* [They are afraid their ship will go down on account of this man.]

> *"And one of them, Caiaphas, being high priest that year, said to them, 'You know nothing at all, nor do you consider that it is expedient for us that one man should die for the people, and not that the whole nation should perish.' Now this he did not say on his own authority; but being high priest that year he prophesied that Jesus would die for the nation, and not for that nation only, but also that He would gather together in one the children of God who were scattered abroad. Then, from that day on, they plotted to put Him to death." —John 11:47-53*

So far, the sailors' actions find a parallel in the leaders of Israel. It is interesting that here the Pharisees take on the persona of heathen Gentiles. One of God's lessons to Jonah is to reveal to him that he is no better than the heathen sailors on the ship and no better than the violent, heathen Ninevites. This is the same lesson we see in the character of the Pharisees, who, like Jonah, become worse examples of Gentiles than the actual Gentiles.

For the rest of the scenario, however, the Gentile sailors describe Pontius Pilate and the Roman authorities. Moving on in the narrative, Jesus is now on trial before the Roman authorities, in whose hands rest the decision to kill Him or not. Again, there is the questioning of Jesus as to Who He is; yet, like Jonah, He remains abnormally quiet through much of the proceedings, offering only a brief explanation.

> *"Then Pilate asked Him, 'Are You the King of the Jews?' He answered and said to him, 'It is as you say.' And the chief priests accused Him of many things, but He answered nothing. Then Pilate asked Him again, saying, 'Do You answer nothing? See how many things they testify against You!' . . ."* (see John 18 for the greater discourse between Pilate and Jesus)

> *"Pilate answered and said to them again, 'What then do you want me to do with Him whom you call the King of the Jews?' So they cried out again, 'Crucify Him!' Then Pilate said to them, 'Why, what evil has He done?' But they cried out all the more, 'Crucify Him!'"—Mark 15:2-4, 12-14*

Pilate finds no reason to condemn this man to death, as the issue is really between Him, His God, and the Jewish nation. Pilate keeps rowing for Jesus against the storm of protest. We should note that the rebellion and anger of the Jews, so like Jonah, is actually orchestrated by God to bring it to this fever pitch as a catalyst for sending Jesus to His death on the cross.

> *"When Pilate saw that he could not prevail at all, but rather that a tumult was rising, he took water and washed his hands before the multitude, saying, 'I am innocent of the blood of this just Person. You see to it.' . . . and led Him away to be crucified."—Matthew 27:24, 31*

Pilate throws Jesus over. Jesus dies and remains in the grave for three days, according to the prophetic sign in Jonah, and is resurrected on the third day. From there, word of His life, death, and resurrection is carried far and wide to many nations, and many Gentiles become believers, as prophesied below:

> *"Indeed He says, 'It is too small a thing that You should be My Servant to raise up the tribes of Jacob, and to restore the preserved ones of Israel; I will also give You as a light to the Gentiles, that You should be My salvation to the ends of the earth.'" —Isaiah 49:6*

> *"The Gentiles shall come to your light, and kings to the brightness of your rising."—Isaiah 60:3*

Scenario 6: A Kingdom Lost

"So Jonah went out of the city and sat on the east side of the city. There he made himself a shelter and sat under it in the shade, till he might see what would become of the city. And the LORD God prepared a plant and made it come up over Jonah, that it might be shade for his head to deliver him from his misery. So Jonah was very grateful for the plant. But as morning dawned the next day God prepared a worm, and it so damaged the plant that it withered. And it happened, when the sun arose, that God prepared a vehement east wind; and the sun beat on Jonah's head, so that he grew faint. Then he wished death for himself, and said, "It is better for me to die than to live."—Jonah 4:5-8

Boiling down the narrative: Not liking the way the Lord deals with his enemies, Jonah goes out of the city to sit by himself. He builds himself a rude booth to provide himself some comfort but is miserable anyway. God comes to him, sees his miserable state, and provides some protection for him in the form of a plant. The man rejoices under his plant-shaded booth. Then the Lord sends a worm, that eats the plant, and the plant dies. Then the Lord send the east wind to scorch the man, making him more miserable than before.

Building Blocks: God, Jonah, Booth, Plant, Worm, East Wind

There are many layers of interpretations to this lesson of the plant, worm, and wind. Because this is an Old Testament picture, we have to consider that God uses physical things like this plant and worm to create a picture of types of people and this may be prophetic of events that will happen in Israel. This illustration is all of these things. Let's begin by setting up the basic relationship between the plant, worm, and wind:

A is to B and C   as   D is to E and F

The plant is to a worm and the east wind as . . .

A, B, and C are physical things with a relationship dynamic between them. D, E, and F represent a parallel relationship between people in a train of events. We have to understand the relationship between the plant, worm, and wind before we can find what **D, E,** and **F** are.

This is where the effort of researching the small pictures associated with these building blocks pays off—so that we know from Scripture what these elements represent. Just to refresh our memories, the plant often represents Israel, God's beautiful but rebellious vine. The plant can also represent any nation that springs up quickly and overruns other nations, glorifies itself, and is cut down by another agent.

In context with the booth, the plant represents God's provision and protection. A man rejoicing under a plant-shaded booth is a picture of the Feast of Tabernacles, which, at its height under Solomon, becomes a picture of the Messianic kingdom to come. Therefore, a man rejoicing under a plant-shaded booth equates to a picture of the kingdom.

The worm is an agent that brings corruption associated with death and is often an agent of judgment divinely appointed to bring destruction. It can also represent something or someone lowly, rejected, or despised.

The east wind is the agent of divine judgment.

Let's plug in some possible substitutions for the plant, worm, and wind.

A is to B is to C   as   D is to E is to F

A plant is to a worm and the east wind as is . . .
(A people) being overtaken by (a destroyer) followed by (judgment).

On a very simplistic level, we can look at Jonah as the plant, and his anger is the worm that eats away at him. His anger robs him of the provision and protection of the Lord, and he is without shield when the Lord sends the scorching east wind.

In a much larger picture, Israel is described as the vine of God's planting that has become corrupted.

> *"Yet I had planted you a noble vine, a seed of highest quality. How then have you turned before Me into the degenerate plant of an alien vine?"*
> —Jeremiah 2:21

In Ezekiel 17, the Lord speaks of rebellious Israel as a spreading plant that is brought under tribute by the King of Babylon. Though the plant was brought low, yet it thrived, but when it rebelled against Babylon by seeking help from Egypt, then the plant was uprooted and sent away into captivity. Thus the plant is facing destruction at the hands of a destroyer and judgment of a punishing east wind. Of the damaged and rebellious nation, the Lord asks:

> *". . . Will it thrive? Will he not pull up its roots, cut off its fruit, and leave it to wither? All of its spring leaves will wither, and no great power or many people will be needed to pluck it up by its roots. Behold, it is planted, will*

it thrive? Will it not utterly wither when the east wind touches it? It will wither in the garden terrace where it grew."—Ezekiel 17:9-10

In this passage, the King of Babylon and east wind become the agents of destruction and judgment, respectively, for the rebellious nation of Israel that is brought low, uprooted, and planted in alien soil, where it fails to thrive, and withers under the east wind.

In similar fashion, rebellious and disobedient Jonah, like the plant, is uprooted from his land and sent to Assyria. The question remains if he will thrive in captivity if he continues in his rebellion. That is a second interpretation that fits the model.

Here is another variation of the relationship dynamic using the plant-shaded booth as a picture of the kingdom.

A plant-covered booth is to a **worm** followed by the **east wind** as is . . . (A picture of a kingdom) being corrupted by (a human agent) then followed by (an act of divine judgment).

The branch-covered booth invokes the imagery of the Feast of Tabernacles, a picture of the kingdom with God in His Temple, the Davidic King on His throne, and all Israel camped about. That picture was supposed to be perpetuated throughout the generations of Israel's kings until Messiah's coming, but the picture becomes corrupted as a whole when a worm eats away at it.

Who is the worm, the human agent that corrupted that picture initially? Jeroboam, king of the northern kingdom of Israel.

Immediately after Solomon dies, the kingdom splits into the kingdom of Israel to the north and the kingdom of Judah to the south. Jeroboam, King of Israel, decides that instead of having all the people return to the Temple in Jerusalem for worship and feasts, he will make his own version of everything—including the Feast of Tabernacles.

"And Jeroboam said in his heart, 'Now the kingdom may return to the house of David: If these people go up to offer sacrifices in the house of the LORD at Jerusalem, then the heart of this people will turn back to their lord, Rehoboam king of Judah, and they will kill me and go back to Rehoboam king of Judah.' Therefore the king asked advice, made two calves of gold, and said to the people, 'It is too much for you to go up to Jerusalem. Here are your gods, O Israel, which brought you up from the land of Egypt!' And he set up one in Bethel, and the other he put in Dan. Now this thing became a sin, for the people went to worship before the one as far as Dan. He made shrines on the high places, and made priests

from every class of people, who were not of the sons of Levi. Jeroboam ordained a feast on the fifteenth day of the eighth month, like the feast that was in Judah, and offered sacrifices on the altar. So he did at Bethel, sacrificing to the calves that he had made. And at Bethel he installed the priests of the high places which he had made. So he made offerings on the altar which he had made at Bethel on the fifteenth day of the eighth month, in the month which he had devised in his own heart. And he ordained a feast for the children of Israel, and offered sacrifices on the altar and burned incense."—1 Kings 12:26-33

Jeroboam, the worm, corrupts the picture of the kingdom represented by the Feast of Tabernacles, eating away at it until the picture withers and dies for the northern kingdom. What followed was the east wind, the scorching judgment that swept from the east in the form of the Assyrian nation, carrying the kingdom of Israel away into captivity.

In the narrative of Jonah, Jonah is a Hebrew prophet from that northern kingdom and representative of disobedient Israel. He rejoices in the kingdom represented by his plant-covered booth while it flourishes but does nothing to help it nor hinder the corruption that damages it. Thus, that kingdom is taken away from him—with all God's provision and protection—and he is made to suffer under the punishment of the scorching east wind in the land of Assyria.

Jonah is living out the prophetic picture of events on the near horizon for the northern kingdom of Israel, of which he is representative. This is a third interpretation of this relationship dynamic.

Thousands of years later, another generation of rebellious Israel listens to Jesus tell a parable of a kingdom that will be torn from the hands of the wicked and disobedient servants of the kingdom (Parable of the Wicked Vinedressers, Matthew 21:33-44). Again there is a relationship between the plant, worm, and east wind elements.

The vineyard owned by the landowner is symbolic of the kingdom and a variation of the plant imagery.

The worm represents the destroyers, the wicked vinedressers who kill, not the vineyard, but the heir of the landowner, and take the vineyard kingdom for themselves. Remember, the plant—the picture of the kingdom—is the totality of God (the landowner), the King (the heir), and the nation of Israel. The wicked vinedressers corrupt that picture by killing the heir.

The east wind is the judgment that follows. This beautiful vineyard is taken away from the wicked vinedressers by the angry landlord. Jesus likens the wicked vinedressers to the chief priests and Pharisees of His day, saying:

> *"Therefore I say to you, the kingdom of God will be taken from you and given to a nation bearing the fruits of it."*—Matthew 21:43

Instead of believing in Jesus and embracing Him as the Messiah King and heir to the kingdom, these servants of the kingdom (the worms) crucify Him, thus corrupting the picture that should have been fulfilled. For this reason, the kingdom is torn from their grasp and the nation is swept away into the Diaspora of the Gentile nations.

So far, the worm is the corrupter or destroyer of the picture of the kingdom. But there is another aspect to that worm. A worm is also a person who is deemed lowly, despised, and rejected, something to be abhorred because of its association with death and the grave.

What happens when the One Who should be considered the beautiful plant, the symbol of God's provision and protection, is wrongly cast in the image of the worm? This is what the Pharisees do to Jesus. They, who are the true worms and His destroyers, look on Him as if He were the worm corrupting the picture of the Messianic King. Though He Himself is not the worm, even so He takes on the persona of the worm, bearing the scorching wrath of divine judgment for the sin of the people, and is consigned to the grave—and yet not to corruption.

The worm mentioned in Jonah 4:7 is specifically the *towla'*, the scarlet worm, which is the source of scarlet dye used in the Old Testament; but more importantly, it is the picture of Christ Himself dying on the cross.

While looking up the meaning of the Hebrew word, *towla'*, in the lexicon concordance in *www.blueletterbible.org*, I found the following description noted with the entry:

> "When the female of the scarlet worm species was ready to give birth to her young, she would attach her body to the trunk of a tree, fixing herself so firmly and permanently that she would never leave again. The eggs deposited beneath her body were thus protected until the larvae were hatched and able to enter their own life cycle. As the mother died, the crimson fluid stained her body and the surrounding wood. From the dead bodies of such female scarlet worms, the commercial scarlet dyes of antiquity were extracted. What a picture this gives of Christ, dying on the tree, shedding his precious blood that he might 'bring many sons unto glory' (Hebrews 2:10)! He died for us, that we might live through him! Psalm 22:6 describes such a worm and gives us this picture of Christ. (cf. Isaiah 1:18)" (Henry Morris. Biblical Basis for Modern

Science, Baker Book House, 1985, p. 73)[1]

In His first coming, Jesus is the tender plant Who became the despised and rejected worm, as Isaiah says:

> *"For He shall grow up before Him as a tender plant, and as a root out of dry ground. He has no form or comeliness; and when we see Him, there is no beauty that we should desire Him. He is despised and rejected by men, a Man of sorrows and acquainted with grief. And we hid, as it were, our faces from Him; He was despised, and we did not esteem Him. Surely He has borne our griefs and carried our sorrows; Yet we esteemed Him stricken, smitten by God, and afflicted."—Isaiah 53:2-4*

The Psalmist carries the picture further.

> *"But I am a worm, and no man; a reproach of men, and despised by the people. All those who see Me ridicule Me; they shoot out the lip, they shake the head, saying, 'He trusted in the LORD, let Him rescue Him; Let Him deliver Him, since He delights in Him!' . . . For dogs have surrounded Me; The congregation of the wicked has enclosed Me. They pierced My hands and My feet; I can count all My bones. They look and stare at Me. They divide My garments among them, and for My clothing they cast lots."*
> *—Psalm 22:6-8, 16-18*

As the *towla'* worm, Jesus dies on the cross so that salvation may be offered to many. He goes down to the grave and yet not to the corruption of the grave.

If we think of the worm as being Christ, then under what circumstances does Christ become the agent for bringing destruction on the plant?

> *"And if anyone hears My words and does not believe, I do not judge him; for I did not come to judge the world but to save the world. He who rejects Me, and does not receive My words, has that which judges him—the word that I have spoken will judge him in the last day."—John 12:47-48*

He is such an agent for those who do not believe. Those who reject Him will wither like the vine and die in their wickedness and corruption, to be cut down and be swept away in burning judgment.

> *"I am the vine, you are the branches. He who abides in Me, and I in him, bears much fruit; for without Me you can do nothing. If anyone does not abide in Me, he is cast out as a branch and is withered; and they gather them and throw them into the fire, and they are burned."—John 15:5-6*

---

1 "H8438 - towla` - Strong's Hebrew Lexicon (KJV)." Blue Letter Bible. Web. 21 Dec, 2018. <https://www.blueletterbible.org/lang/lexicon/lexicon.cfm?Strongs=H8438&t=KJV>.

> *". . . Because of unbelief they were broken off, and you stand by faith. Do not be haughty, but fear. For if God did not spare the natural branches, He may not spare you either. Therefore consider the goodness and severity of God: on those who fell, severity; but toward you, goodness, if you continue in His goodness. Otherwise you also will be cut off."—Romans 11:20-22*

Keep in mind, the Lord prepares both the plant and the worm for their roles in this illustration. In Jesus' case, the corruption of the picture was ordained, as was the work of the worm—even Jesus Himself becoming a worm consigned to the grave—so that His death on the cross and resurrection might be accomplished and thus provide the means of salvation for all men. God orchestrates the unreasoning anger in the Jewish people to accomplish Jesus' death so that many would be saved.

Understanding this aspect of the picture lends another dimension to the exchange between God and Jonah. Jonah is angered beyond reason at the loss of that single plant, but God orchestrates Jonah's anger up to the point of the plant's death, so that the anger would be unreasoning. Thus, the Lord turns it into a lesson, rebuking Jonah for not being angry with the loss of an entire people in need of saving on the eve of their destruction. Is it better for one man to suffer and die to save the many, or for all to be lost?

So you can see, the relationship dynamic between plant, worm, and wind offers a number of possible interpretations, depending on which aspect of the elements we use as building blocks.

Scenario 7: The Grand Picture

The entire book of Jonah encompasses the grand picture of Israel's history from her calling to her current condition of being left in the Diaspora. In the following chart, I outline the elements of the narrative as they apply to Jonah (left of center) and then make the same parallels to Israel (right of center), of which Jonah is representative.

Each begins with a calling from God, and both quickly turn to disobedience and rebellion. Working through the narrative in Part 1, I point out that Jonah begins down the path of idolatry as he seeks a life apart from God. The same plays out in Israel's history to a much greater extent.

In both cases, God deals with the disobedience by sending Jonah and Israel alike into exile—Jonah into the fish and Israel into Assyria and Babylon. The exile produces the necessary repentance and turning. A return to God effects a return to the Land of Israel. The covenant and commandment are renewed, and both Jonah and Israel respond with obedience, but the obedience is in form only—out of obligation and not from a heart for God.

At a certain point, both Jonah and Israel find themselves again surrounded by Gentiles. Jonah stands in the midst of the Ninevites. Israel is overrun by the Roman Empire. There God engages each in some personal interaction. He comes to Jonah as Himself; but to Israel, He takes on human form as Jesus Christ, the Son of God.

Even as Chapters 1–3 etch Israel's history from their beginning until the time of Christ, they do dual duty in sketching the picture of Christ as His ministry begins—His baptism and temptations. Jonah 4 then starts the convergence of both Israel and Christ as they face off.

Just as God comes to address the heart of Jonah, so Jesus comes to assess and correct the wrong heart attitude of God's children. Just as God reasons with Jonah, so Jesus begins to reason with the people and the religious leaders of His day. Twice the unbelieving religious leaders seek a sign from Him and He responds by telling them no sign will be given except the sign of Jonah (Matthew 12:38-41, Matthew 16:1-4). The answer lies in Jonah.

Just as God expresses His compassion for Nineveh, which He sees as a kingdom of little children, so Jesus blesses the little children, saying of such is the kingdom of heaven (Matthew 19:13-14). Jesus uses the illustration of a little child to deliver a warning to those who would cause those of child-like faith to stumble, saying:

> "But whoever causes one of these little ones who believe in Me to stumble,

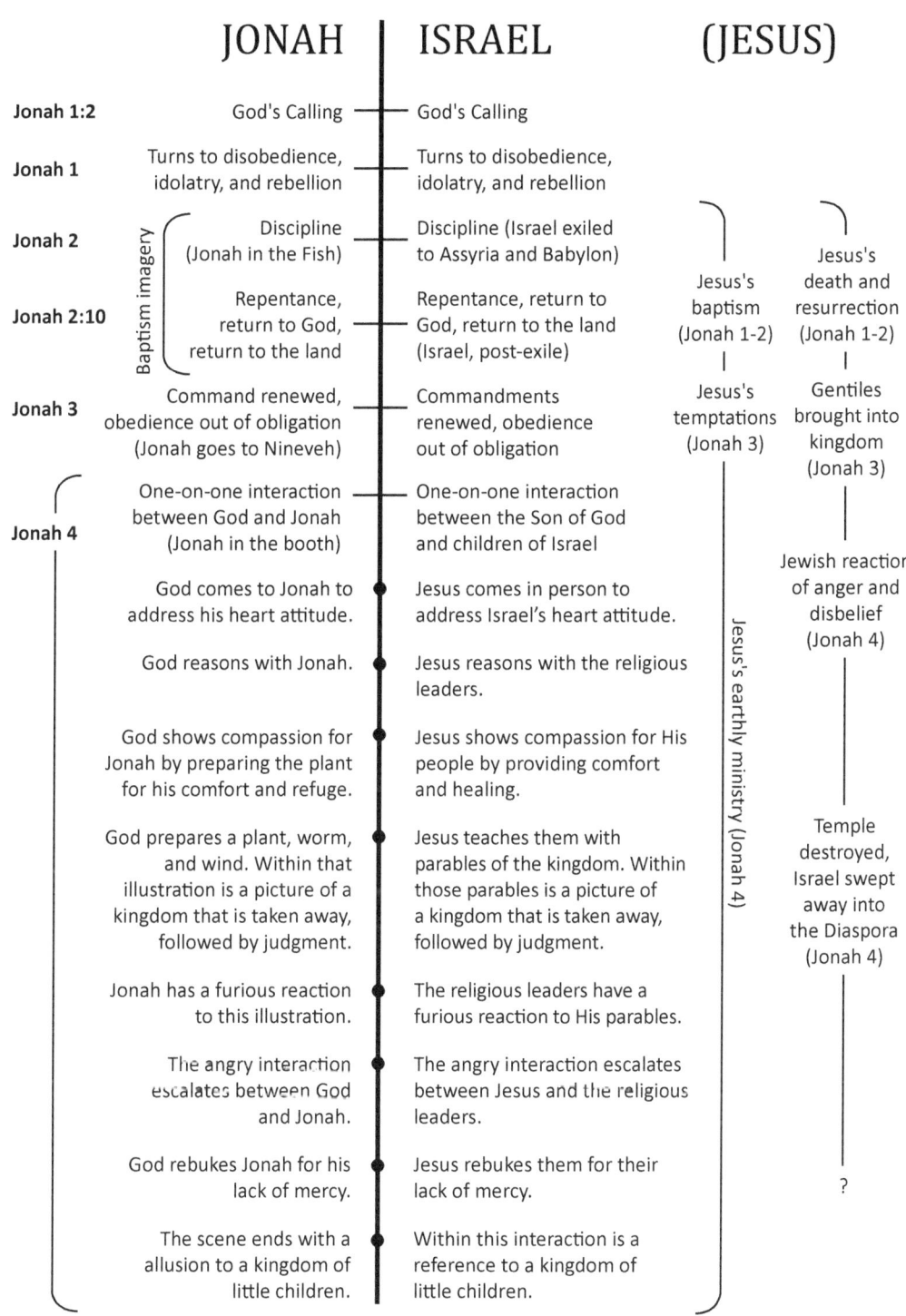

Pictures of Christ in Jonah | 149

> *it would be better for him if a millstone were hung around his neck, and he were thrown into the sea."—Mark 9:42*

Just as God prepares the plant, worm, and wind illustration for Jonah, so Jesus teaches in parables about a kingdom (Matthew 13, 18, 20, 21). Repeatedly, He warns that the kingdom will be torn from the hands of wicked and corrupt servants. The parable of the wicked vine-dressers (Matthew 21) particularly enrages the religious leaders.

Jesus also makes an interesting lesson with a fig tree (Mark 11:13-21). He comes to a fig tree, which has many leaves but has produced no fruit. At Jesus' command, it begins to wither. According to the Gospel of Mark, this incident is immediately followed by the cleansing of the Temple, as Jesus falls furiously upon the moneychangers and drives them out of the Temple. There is an echo of Jonah's withering plant about the scene, as the beautiful Temple—that should have been a house of prayer—is corrupted by the moneylenders who have turned it to a den of theives. Christ's fury pours out like the east wind, yet the corruption in the Temple is systemic. We know from history that this Temple will be swept away by the Romans in 70 A.D.

Like Jonah's blinding anger toward God, the fury of the religious leaders escalates into a blinding desire to kill Jesus. Jesus' response also escalates as He answers with woes upon them and rebukes them, particularly for their lack of mercy on the people (Matthew 23).

It would seem that the scenario between Jesus and the religious leaders ends in a stalemate if the parallel were to end at Jonah 4:11. But the scenario doesn't end there. From Jonah 4, we return to the events surrounding the sign of Jonah in Jonah 1–3, and a second pass is made through the narrative, this time beginning with Jesus' death (which He describes as a baptism).

Just as the narrative picks up again with Jonah on trial before the sailors, so we pick up with the conversation over what to do with Jesus and his trial before Pilate. All that plays out as we discussed earlier in Scenario 5 with His death and resurrection. The word of His death and resurrection spreads to the Gentile world, and many Gentiles come to faith, just as the sailors and Ninevites did.

Yet there is a reaction to this among the Jews that mimics Jonah's reaction to the Ninevites. They are angry and bewildered when the kingdom events do not play out as they imagine or desire. Many are unwilling to accept God's will concerning the Gentiles.

In 70 A.D., even as the Gentile nations are being brought into the kingdom, the Romans destroy the physical Temple and the wind of judgment carries the Jewish people into the Diaspora (another variation of the plant/worm/wind illustration). Like Jonah's end, the resolution of Israel's heart remains in question to this day.

God's Glory in the Earthen Vessel

CONCLUSION

When you begin to sort through the overlapping pictures in Jonah, you can appreciate the confusion of the Jews in Jesus' day in trying to identify who was who. Jonah is never just one person following one narrative. Depending on which building blocks of imagery are being combined, he represents a number of characters in various settings.

Imagine now if you did not know the end picture. How would you sort out the elements and know which building blocks create which picture to be fulfilled? Do we, who know the final picture of Christ in His first coming, recognize the picture within the picture of Jonah?

In Jonah 1–3, Jonah is thoroughly intertwined in the figures of Jesus and John the Baptist. Then there is the image of the *yownah*, the dove, added to the mix, who is Jonah and yet not Jonah.

As the man asleep on the boat in a storm, is Jesus likened to Jonah or God? How is it possible He can be both? How can the Gentile King of Nineveh portray a Messianic King?

How can the same passage speak of a literal baptism and a death?

Who is the plant and who is the worm? How can the plant and the worm be the same figure?

Who would have thought that Messiah's story would loop twice within the same narrative? How can that imagery replay over and over in history the way it does?

There is no one definitive scenario.

I admit myself humbled by the depth and breadth of the picture of Christ in the book of Jonah. It is marvelous and speaks to the surpassing glory of a magnificent, omniscient, omnipotent God.

Only a God of such glory can orchestrate events in the life of a man like Jonah for His purpose. God lets Jonah's own volition and base character drive the unfolding events, and adds only what is essential—the storm, the fish, the plant, the worm, and the wind—to bring Jonah to the particular choices he is given in responding to those events. Even when this disobedient man responds by making the most rebellious, selfish, emotion-driven choices, God uses every one of those choices to bring glory to Himself.

Remember, this is Jonah, the exceedingly flawed earthen vessel through whom God puts His glory on display. This is selfish, self-focused, unmerciful Jonah, who struggles with anger, prejudice, and hate, and is determined to follow his own path, even when it takes him downward into the darkest of places. This is a man who claims to have a relationship with God yet denies God's sovereignty over his life, who struggles with God's will as an ambassador of mercy.

Every step of Jonah's obedience and disobedience is turned to God's advantage. It is God Who receives the glory in the lives of the sailors and the Ninevites, not Jonah.

It is to God's glory that Jonah is brought to a point of deep brokenness in his life, yet not completely destroyed. Paul describes God's mercy and grace in this text:

> *"We are hard-pressed on every side, yet not crushed; we are perplexed, but not in despair; persecuted, but not forsaken; struck down, but not destroyed—always carrying about in the body the dying of the Lord Jesus, that the life of Jesus also may be manifested in our body. For we who live are always delivered to death for Jesus' sake, that the life of Jesus also may be manifested in our mortal flesh."—2 Corinthians 4:8-11*

It is to God's glory that such an earthen vessel as Jonah portrays in himself the picture of the dying of the Lord Jesus, and that the life of Jesus is manifested through Jonah in a way that shows the excellence of God's power, not Jonah's.

Even so, we are not called to follow Jonah's example in this.

While God can use even the most flawed vessel for His purpose, we cannot use that as an excuse for pursuing sinful, selfish behavior, thinking that God will use it for good regardless. We are called to bear witness of Christ through a life of obedience and righteousness, not disobedience and wickedness, as Paul exhorts us in Romans 3. If we are hard-pressed, perplexed, persecuted, and struck down, it should not be as punishment for our own sin. In that final confrontation over the plant, worm, and wind, we see how God uses Jonah's unrighteousness to demonstrate His own righteousness; and He was not unjust for inflicting a measure of wrath and judgment on Jonah for his lack of mercy. God's glory will shine through His people, either through our praise and thanksgiving or through our rebuke and breaking.

Even so, if God can work His purpose through the life of someone like Jonah and show mercy to wicked Ninevites, does not a great hope remain for us?

We are the earthen vessels. It is the glory of God at work in us and through us—His power tempered by His grace and mercy—that humbles us, lifts us up above our frailties, and gives us hope, reminding us that only by His power do we live and have purpose. That is, perhaps, the greatest lesson we can take from Jonah.

May the Lord's mercy endure forever.

www.ingramcontent.com/pod-product-compliance
Lightning Source LLC
Chambersburg PA
CBHW060423010526
44118CB00017B/2335